Into Your Hands, Father

WILFRID STINISSEN

Into Your Hands, Father

Abandoning Ourselves to the God Who Loves Us

Translated by
Sister Clare Marie, O.C.D.

IGNATIUS PRESS   SAN FRANCISCO

Original Swedish edition:
Fader, jag överlämnar mig åt dig
© 1986 by Karmeliterna Tågarp Glumslöv, Tågarp

English translation made by permission of the author

Cover art:
Crucifixion. Byzantine mosaic;
Baptistery, Florence, Italy
Scala/Art Resource, N.Y.

Cover designed by Riz Boncan Marsella

© 2011 by Ignatius Press, San Francisco
All rights reserved
ISBN 978-1-58617-477-4
Library of Congress Control Number 2010931418
Printed in the United States of America ∞

Contents

Father,

I abandon myself
into Your hands;
do with me what You will.
For whatever You may do I thank You.

I am ready for all,
I accept all.

Let only Your will be done in me
as in all Your creatures.
I wish no more than this, O Lord.

Into Your hands
I commend my soul.
I offer it to You
with all the love of my heart.
For I love You, my God,
and so need to give myself,
to surrender myself
into Your hands,
without reserve,
and with boundless confidence,
for You are my Father.

—Brother Charles of Jesus
   (1858–1916)

Preface

The Gospels and spiritual literature point out various practices of importance on the journey to God. We are told to deny ourselves, forgive one another, carry our cross, fast, and give alms. We must also love our neighbor, pray with others and in private, bring our troubles to the Lord, and be peacemakers. All of these things have their place, and nothing may be overlooked, but they may cause us to feel confused and divided, and we might even ask ourselves where we will find the strength to do all that is required. In spiritual reading we are instructed about balanced asceticism, the Mass readings of the day tell of prayer, and the retreat master speaks about love. We are pulled in different directions, and, instead of finding peace, we become restless. What we need most is a central idea, something so basic and comprehensive that it encompasses everything else.

In my opinion that central idea is surrender. One might expect a Carmelite to place prayer at the center. That is what Saint Teresa of Avila and Saint John of the Cross did. But there is another well-known Carmelite, Saint Thérèse of Lisieux, who was totally fascinated by surrender. "Now abandonment alone guides me, I have no other compass! I can no longer ask for anything with fervor except the accomplishment of God's will in my soul."[1] "Jesus deigned to show me the road that leads to this Divine Furnace, and this road is the surrender of the little child who sleeps without fear in its Father's arms."[2]

A few years ago, my brother and I visited a Trappist monastery in Bricquebec, France. The monastery's subprior told us of the spiritual journey of the old abbot Dom Vital Lehodey. In the beginning he was completely absorbed by the liturgy, as one would expect of a Trappist monk. Gradually, he discovered interior prayer and wrote his well-known book *The Ways of Mental Prayer* (*Les Voies de l'oraison mentale*), which can be found in most monastery libraries. In the end, he found an even simpler and straighter path and wrote his equally well-known book *Holy Abandonment* (*Le Saint Abandon*). This concept does not contradict the teaching of either Saint Teresa or Saint John of the Cross. If one reads their description of union carefully, one notices that this total abandonment is what constitutes the very essence of union with God.

The life of Jesus shows that it is acceptable to choose surrender as a unifying idea. According to the letter to the Hebrews, he says upon entering the world: " 'Behold, I have come to do your will, O God,' as it is written of me in the roll of the book"

[1] Thérèse of Lisieux, *Story of a Soul*, trans. John Clarke, O.C.D. (Washington D.C.: ICS Publications, 1976), p. 178.

[2] Ibid., p. 188.

(Heb 10:7), and he finishes his life with an act of absolute surrender: "Father, into your hands I commit my spirit!" (Lk 23:46). Abandonment is truly the alpha and omega in his life.

We can distinguish between three degrees or stages in surrender. The first stage consists in accepting and assenting to God's will as it manifests itself in all the circumstances of life. The second is actively doing God's will at every moment of life. In the third stage, one is so completely abandoned to God that one has become a pliant tool in his hands. Now it is no longer *I* who do God's will, but *God* who accomplishes his will through me. In Saint Thérèse's words: "For a long time, I have no longer belonged to myself, I am totally surrendered to Jesus, so He is free to do with me as He wills."[3]

---

[3] Thérèse de Lisieux, "Manuscrit C", in *Oeuvres complètes* (Paris: Éditions du Cerf, Desclée de Brouwer, 1998), p. 248.

I

Accepting God's Will

A problem many people have today is that they no longer recognize God's will in everything that happens. They no longer believe in a Providence that allows *all* that takes place to work for the good of those who love God (Rom 8:28). They say all too easily and superficially: "But it is not God's will that there are wars or that people starve or are persecuted. . . ." No, it is not God's will that human beings fight with each other. He wills that we love one another. But when evil people who are opposed to his will hate and murder others, he allows this to become a part of his plan for them. We must distinguish between the actual deed of someone who, for example, slanders us and the situation that comes to us as a result of the deed, which was not God's will. God did not will the sinful act, but from all eternity he has taken into account the consequences of it in our lives. He wills that we grow through those very things that others do to us that are difficult and painful.

There is a deeply rooted tendency in human beings to look at others and their failings. In doing this, we miss what is most essential: to accept and assent to

13

God's will in our lives, a will that is largely formed
by the opposition of others to God's will. We need
only look at Jesus. It was not the Father's will that his
Son be killed, nor did he inspire anyone to kill him.
He did will, however, that Jesus would freely be the
sacrifice for the sins of mankind. He willed that Jesus
would let himself be put to death. Jesus did not say,
as we often hear today: "But this is not God's will,
this cannot be God's will." He said: "Abba, Father, all
things are possible to you; remove this chalice from
me; yet not what I will, but what you will" (Mk
14:36). For every one of us there is a chalice that the
Father offers us to drink. We have difficulty recognizing it as coming from him, since a great deal of
its contents comes from other people. Nevertheless,
it is the Father who asks us to drink the bitter cup.
It was so for Jesus, and it is the same for us.

"Your Providence, O Father, Guides!" (*cf. Wis 14:3*)

God has everything in his hand. Nothing exists outside the sphere of his influence. Nothing can upset
his plans. Augustine formulates this very radically:
"Nothing happens that the Almighty does not will
should happen, either by permitting it or by himself
doing it."[1] To let something happen is also a decision
of God.

---

[1] *Enchiridion de fide, spe et caritate*, no. 24.

That God *allows* so much to happen is a great stumbling block for us. Why is he so passive? Why does he not intervene? How is Auschwitz possible and the torture chamber and the threat of a horrible nuclear war if God is concerned with us? These questions torment us and are not easy to answer. In chapter 2, I will return to this and try to show why God endowed human beings with free will, though he knew that this very freedom would pave the way for terrible catastrophes.

Let us limit ourselves for now to the undeniable fact that the Father did not prevent the painful death of his only-begotten Son. This fact is a kind of archetype, which shows us two things very clearly. The first is that suffering and even total ruin do not signify a lack of love on the part of the Father. The second is that suffering is not in vain; it bears fruit and has redeeming power. Since Jesus has gone through it, suffering has become an instrument of salvation. This applies not only to suffering that is borne generously and heroically. Who knows how we would react in the torture chamber? It is enough that we *try* as best we can to accept suffering or that we merely allow whatever comes our way to happen. The Church regards the Holy Innocents as martyrs, even though they never consciously or willingly consented to their violent deaths.

God makes use of evil in such a superb way and with such skill that the result is better than if there had never been evil. For those of us who find ourselves in the midst of evil, this is not easy to swallow. We think that the price to be paid for these good results is far too high. But Saint Paul rejoices when he ponders the "mystery", God's magnificent plan, "hidden for ages in God" (Eph 3:9), where evil and sin also have their place. "God has consigned all men to disobedience, that he may have mercy upon all" (Rom 11:32). In this daring passage, which, strictly speaking, seems somewhat questionable, since it seems to place the initiative of sin on God, Saint Paul assures us that even the greatest catastrophe, namely, sin, contributes to the revelation of love. Nothing falls outside of God's plan. That is why the tragedy of the world, despite all its terror, has no definitive character. All the absurdity of which mankind's foolishness and blindness are capable is caught up in God's loving omnipotence. He is able to fit even the absurd into his plan of salvation and thereby give it meaning.

In his stories about Hasidism, Martin Buber writes: "On the evening before Yom Kippur, the great day of atonement, Rabbi Susa once heard the cantor singing in the synagogue in a wonderful way: 'and it is forgiven.' He then called out to God: 'Lord of the universe, this song could never have resounded in your presence had Israel not sinned.' "[2]

"There is indeed much done against God's will by

---

[2] *Die Erzählungen der Chassidim* (Zurich: Manesse Verlag, 1949), p. 387.

evil men," Augustine writes, "but his wisdom and power are so great that everything seemingly contrary to it, in reality, works toward the good outcome or end that he has preordained."[3] In other words: "God accomplishes his good will through the evil will of others. In this way the Father's loving plan was realized . . . and Jesus suffered death for our sake."[4]

There is no need to distinguish carefully between what God positively wills and what he merely permits. What he permits is also a part of his universal, all-embracing will. He has foreseen it from the beginning and decided how he will use it. Everything that happens has a purpose in God's plan. He is so good that all that comes in contact with him becomes in some way good. God's goodness is contagious and even gives evil something of its own goodness. "God is so good", Augustine says, "that in his hand, even evil brings about good. He would never have permitted evil to occur if he had not, thanks to his perfect goodness, been able to use it."[5] Who can dare to speak of chance? "Nothing in our lives happens haphazardly. . . . Everything that takes place against our will can only come from God's will, his Providence, the order he has created, the permission he gives, and the laws he has established."[6]

[3] *De civitate Dei* 22, 2, 1.
[4] *Enchiridion*, no. 26.
[5] *Opus imperf. contra Julianum*, lib. 5, no. 60.
[6] *Enarrationes in Ps 118*, v. 12.

The distinction between what God wills and what he merely permits is extremely important on the theological level. When it has to do with real life, however, with unavoidable events and our reaction to them, we might wonder if speculation about the difference is not often a subtle form of escapism. If God does not will the evil that befalls me, I do not need to accept it. Then I may in good conscience rebel against it.

Job is not interested in such distinctions. The evil that afflicts him comes directly from the devil. Nevertheless, Job says: "The LORD gave and the LORD has taken away; blessed be the name of the LORD!" (Job 1:21). Father Jean-Pierre de Caussade (1675–1751) writes to Sister Marie-Henriette de Bousmard: "Be profoundly persuaded that nothing takes place in this world either spiritually or physically, that God does not will, or at least, permit; therefore we ought no less to submit to the permissions of God in things that do not depend on us, than to His absolute will."[7]

A Way to Live Continually in God's Presence

If God is the creator of heaven and earth and the great director guiding the drama of the world and mankind, then I can encounter him everywhere. He pours out his love upon me in and through all that

[7] Rev. Jean-Pierre de Caussade, S.J., Letters, in *Abandonment to Divine Providence* (Exeter: Sidney Lee, Catholic Records Press, 1921), p. 127.

happens. "Open your mouth wide, and I will fill it" (Ps 81:10). I do not need to consider when it is wise to open my mouth and when it is better to close it. I will always have my mouth wide open. I live in a land where milk and honey flow. At every moment I receive wonderful and substantial food. It does not always taste like honey, to be sure. Sometimes it seems bitter, but we know that what is bitter is often the most wholesome. God's action fills the entire universe, and I may surrender to it and let myself be carried by its waves.

We seek God, but in reality he does not need to be sought. He is everywhere. We can never escape him. Everything speaks of him, and everything mediates something of him. We do not need to go long distances or buy a compass to find the right way. God is in our everyday reality: our parents, our body with its health or sickness, our gifts and limitations, our riches, our poverty, and our high or low IQ. As soon as we cease to resist all of this and open ourselves to accept God's reality, we begin to live in his kingdom.

Even modern psychology has a dim realization that it is vitally important for people to accept their own characteristics and not wish to be someone else. The psychotherapist does not aim primarily at teaching the patient new patterns or ways of behavior. He wants to help the patient to accept himself and no longer deny or repress the past, but rather to integrate it. The transformation comes almost of itself as a result of this complete acceptance. But it is difficult for us to accept our fate when we do not know God is behind it and that it is through this very fate that he was and is real in our lives. That is why psychology's capacity is limited and can never lead to total liberation.

Wherever we go, we encounter God. When we begin to realize this, we recognize ourselves in Jacob's "aha" experience. He wakes from sleep and exclaims: "Surely the LORD is in this place; and I did not know it. . . . How awesome is this place! This is none other than the house of God, and this is the gate of heaven!" (Gen 28:16–17). The dream of the ladder that reached up to the heavens and on which God's angels walked up and down made Jacob realize there is contact between heaven and earth and that angels come continually with messages from heaven. Instead of events that are commonplace and dull, we now meet angels.

Most Christians, however, resemble the disciples who saw Jesus walking on the lake but believed they were seeing a ghost. Even Mary Magdalen was mistaken and believed she was seeing the gardener, when it was nevertheless the Lord who was revealing himself. If only we were like the bride in the Song of Songs who recognized him at a great distance: "The voice of my beloved! Behold, he comes, leaping upon the mountains. . . . Behold, there he stands behind our wall, gazing in at the windows, looking through the lattice" (Song 2:8–9).

How can you know that you are living in God's will? This is the sign: If you are troubled about anything, that means you are not completely abandoned to God's will. The one who lives according to God's will is not troubled about anything. If he needs something, he surrenders it and even himself to the Lord. He places it in his hands. If he does not get what he needs, he remains calm, as though he had received it. He is not afraid, whatever happens, for he knows that it is God's will. When he is afflicted with illness, he thinks: I need this sickness, otherwise God would not have sent it. He thus preserves peace in body and soul.[8]

This text by the Russian Starets Silvan (1866–1938), whose holiness is widely recognized in the Orthodox Church, can be used as a test. Does it make us happy or angry when we read it? If we feel angry, it is perhaps because we do not see things that happen in the right context, namely, as material in God's hands, which he uses to carry out his plans. It is irrelevant to God whether the material is good or bad in itself. It is enough that he touches it for it to become a suitable tool.

This is also true for us. We try to prove our skill by making something beautiful with poor materials. Give the most expensive and finest foodstuffs to a beginner in the art of cooking, and he will prepare

[8] Silouane, *Écrits spirituels*, Spiritualité orientale 5 (Abbaye de Bellefontaine, 1976), pp. 47–48.

an awful dinner with it. One who has mastered the art, on the other hand, can prepare an appetizing meal even with leftovers. Here on earth there are limits, of course. We are not able to make a good dinner out of bad food, but God is! We can sit down at table and eat whatever he serves without being troubled or afraid. It is always healthy and substantial fare! It is always a feast, since God offers himself in all that he wills and does.

Seen in this way, the omnipresence of God takes on a whole new meaning. His presence is not static or passive. He is not a weak spectator who witnesses how people misuse their freedom and destroy his plans. It would be senseless to surrender oneself to such a powerless God. God is active love, and all that occurs and is done by human beings is integrated into his all-encompassing activity. We swim in it.

I should die of thirst rushing like this from one fountain to another, from one stream to another when there is a sea at hand, the waters of which encompass me on every side. All that happens to me therefore will be food for my nourishment, water for my cleansing, fire for my purification, and a channel of grace for all my needs. That which I might endeavor to find in other ways seeks me incessantly and gives itself to me through all creatures. O Love of God! How is it that all creatures do not know how freely you lavish Yourself and Your favors on them while they are seeking You in byways and corners where You are not to be found? How foolish to refuse to breathe the open air, to search for a spot on which to place the foot when there is the whole countryside before you; to be unable to find water when there is a deluge at your service, not to possess and enjoy God, nor to recognize His action when it is present in all things.[9]

There is not a single moment when God is not communicating himself to us. Most of what occurs in our lives seems to happen accidentally and at random. Now and then God reveals his presence. At times we see the thread and we thank him, but he is *always* there; *everything* speaks of him. There is an unbroken continuity in God's action. "He who keeps you will not slumber. Behold, he who keeps Israel will neither slumber nor sleep" (Ps 121:3–4). We sleep for the most part. Yes, our faith sleeps. We do not notice anything extraordinary. In reality, everything is extraordinary. Perhaps the secret can be found in certain saints who died young and who came an incredibly long way in a short time. Not a moment of their lives was lost. Nothing that happened was in vain. They knew that at every moment, in every event and circumstance, not the least in that which seemed to destroy their "spiritual life", God gave them a little push on the back, and they let themselves be pushed by him.

There can be so much escapism in our striving for a "spiritual life". We often flee from the concrete,

---

[9] De Caussade, *Abandonment to Divine Providence*, p. 32.

apparently banal reality that is filled with God's presence to an artificial existence that corresponds with our own ideas of piety and holiness but where God is not present. As long as we want to decide for ourselves where we will find God, we need not fear that we shall meet him! We will meet only ourselves, a touched-up version of ourselves. Genuine spirituality begins when we are prepared to die. Could there be a quicker way to die than to let God form our lives from moment to moment and continually to consent to his action?

Faith: Seeing the Invisible (Heb 11:27)

We have been given new eyes to discover the divine reality, namely, our faith. Faith sees through the outer shell and penetrates to the substance of things. Many Christians think faith is something that has to do with an ethereal world, a gift that enables us to reach another part of reality. It is true that reality becomes greater and wider for one who believes. Faith reveals new areas of reality (the Trinity, angels, and so on), but faith also enables us to see everything we encounter in a completely new way. It sees the deep dimension of daily events. That is why there is no longer anything ordinary for the believer; nothing is uninteresting or boring. Everything becomes exciting and fascinating.

Beautiful thoughts and theories often remain in our heads and do not change our lives. They are not our most important teachers. We are influenced by events. In Hebrew, the term for "word" and "event" (*dabar*) is the same. God speaks through events. When he speaks through his Son, the greatest event in history takes place: the Incarnation. Every event is a word of God to us. He is in everything that happens. I live in God's presence when I accept what happens as a message from him without rebelling against it. I am aware that he is continually working to form and sculpt me. This does not require many thoughts or words. Even work that demands all of my attention does not prevent me from living in God's presence in this way. The only thing necessary is a "yes" attitude; letting God create me.

Anyone who tries to live in this way will experience that it is not easy. Perhaps it would not be so difficult if God created us directly, without using other people and events, but it requires a deep faith to recognize him in everyday, ordinary incidents. The Incarnation has always been the great stumbling block. God and human beings are always just missing each other. We seek him in the great things, but he communicates and reveals himself in the small. "By this you know the Spirit of God", Saint John writes: "every spirit which confesses that Jesus Christ has come in the flesh is of God, and every spirit which does not confess Jesus is not of God. This is the spirit of antichrist" (1 Jn 4:2–3). Even in the early Church, there were many who found it difficult to believe that God could be so human. It is true they believed in a heavenly Christ, but they could not accept that he had anything to do with Jesus of Nazareth. Something of this heresy exists among many of us. A symptom of it is the difficulty we have in recognizing a saint among our acquaintances unless he does something sensational. A person with whom we associate daily and whom we see in his ordinary humanity cannot be a saint! In order to be a saint, one must be either dead or far away. Distance enables us to disregard the small, ordinary, and human and turn it into something great, a myth.

It is important and even necessary to interrupt our work now and then throughout the day and turn to God within us, to speak a few "words of light and love" to him. My faith teaches me that Christ lives in my heart (Eph 3:17) and that I can find him there. It requires a greater amount of faith, however, to recognize God in everything that happens. It is more difficult to see him in a person who frequently disturbs me by calling on the phone at impossible hours than to pause now and then during my work to recollect myself in prayer. But if I do not try to do the first, then the second is not worth very much, either. A God whom I meet only within myself, but not in people and events, is not really incarnate. A dangerous dualism arises from this: contact with God is reduced to a few special moments, while life in gen-

eral is "godless". God is not limited to any particular time. We can be tempted to believe that God
was especially active during the time of which the
Bible speaks, namely, apart from the creation narra-
tives, about two thousand years. What we read in the
Bible, however, is only a small part of sacred history,
which has been going on since the beginning of the
world and will continue until its end. God has chosen
a few moments and illuminated them in a special way
so we might understand that he guides all of history
and is with mankind from beginning to end. Reading
the Bible can teach us that history is always sacred and
that no matter how much people believe, they can act
independently of God, but that it is nevertheless he
who directs and carries all of history. He is present
in everything that happens. Our life is a continuation
of this sacred history. The Bible gives a brief description of the beginning of history (the creation narra-
tives) and the end (the Book of Revelation: the final
and decisive struggle between light and darkness) so
we might grasp that everything that happens between
the beginning and the end is included in this sacred
history. It is not possible to describe everything, for
". . . were every one of them to be written, I suppose
that the world itself could not contain the books that
would be written" (Jn 21:25).

Sacred history continues, and God is writing it
through the lives of each and every one of us. The
most important thing is that we believe it is he who is
writing the book of our lives and that we allow him

to write. We do not need to understand completely what he is writing. Neither could the holy authors who wrote under the inspiration of the Holy Spirit understand all that the Spirit meant. It would be revealed at the proper time. Always wishing to find out God's exact meaning in an episode in our lives is spiritual curiosity. The essential thing is to know *that* God means something *with all that happens* and to live in such openness and wakefulness that he can give us insight into the meaning when he wills.

"You Have Turned My Mourning into Dancing" (Ps 30:11)

We often tend to blame others or circumstances if we do not go forward on the spiritual journey. I do not have time for prayer, I have too much work, I live in a stressful environment, the children are so noisy, I do not get any support in my parish, my religious brothers or sisters do not understand me, I have no spiritual director . . . The list goes on and on.

If we really believe that God is our Father and that he has everything in his hand, we know there is nothing that can hinder us on the way. (Brother Charles de Foucauld's prayer begins with "Father". If that first word is left out, the whole prayer is incomplete.)

> Who shall separate us from the love of Christ? Shall tribulation, or distress, or persecution, or famine, or nakedness, or peril, or sword? . . . No, in all these things we are more than conquerors through him

who loved us. For I am sure that neither death, nor life, nor angels, nor principalities, nor things present, nor things to come, nor powers, nor height, nor depth, nor anything else in all creation, will be able to separate us from the love of God in Christ Jesus our Lord. (Rom 8:35–39)

The life of Jesus is an excellent example of how what appeared to be an obstacle was in fact an effective means. The Pharisees, who rejected Jesus and wanted to prevent him from appearing as the Messiah, were the very ones who, by resisting and killing him, led him to his goal. His goal was, of course, the Cross. Those who nailed him to it did not realize that they were serving God's purposes. In God's hands, our very enemies are the ones who benefit us most. The fish that tried to devour Tobit became sustenance for him and the angel guiding him and even supplied medicine for them (Tob 6:3–6).[10] Perhaps you believe that if a certain enemy who persecutes you disappeared, you would find peace and finally be able to pray. But God uses just this person to deepen your peace, so that it is no longer dependent on external circumstances but finds its foundation in God. Thus, your enemies become your friends.

In the "Precautions" of Saint John of the Cross, he exhorts a brother to regard all the brothers in community as God's artisans, with the task of forming him.

[10] Ibid., p. 87.

The first precaution is to understand that you have come to the monastery so that all may fashion you and try you. Thus, to free yourself from the imperfections and disturbances that can be engendered by the mannerisms and attitudes of the religious and draw profit from every occurrence, you should think that all in the community are artisans—as indeed they are —present there in order to prove you; that some will fashion you with words, others by deeds, and others with thoughts against you; and that in all this you must be submissive as is the statue to the craftsman who molds it, to the artist who paints it, and to the gilder who embellishes it.

If you fail to observe this precaution, you will not know how to overcome your sensitiveness and feelings, nor will you get along well in the community with the religious, nor attain holy peace, nor free yourself from many stumbling blocks and evils.[11]

In some way all people are God's servants. All serve the same end. The irony of fate, or better said, God's humor, arranges that those who resist him most often serve him best. In many lives of the saints, we read about some difficult or even evil person who provides the amount of persecution that seems necessary to make someone a saint. But a characteristic of heaven is its universal gratitude. There everyone is grateful, both to those who showed him love on earth and to those who were his persecutors. Every-

---

[11] John of the Cross, "The Precautions", no. 15, in *The Collected Works of Saint John of the Cross* (Washington, D.C.: I.C.S. Publications, 1979), p. 660.

one did his part, willingly or unwillingly, to realize God's plan.

We may not draw the conclusion from this that we can be indifferent to all that happens. The freedom from cares of which the Gospel speaks is not the same as indifference. Jesus wept over Jerusalem. His sorrow was not for himself but for the inhabitants of Jerusalem. The cares from which he wants to free us are mainly those that revolve around ourselves. A large part of our cares consist of these. To feel sorrow that so few people open themselves to God and dare to trust him is not really worry or something that gives unrest. Tears of this kind well up from love, and such tears are always sweet.

"As Having Nothing, and Yet Possessing Everything" (2 Cor 6:10)

Believing that God can also use and transform our inner poverty is perhaps the most difficult for us. Nevertheless, this poverty can become God's most faithful servant. "The horse produces manure in the stall", writes Tauler (1300–1361).

> In itself, manure is repulsive and pollutes the air. However, the same horse bears it with much toil to the fields, where it produces a precious harvest of fine wheat or excellent wine, a harvest that would not have been so good if it had not received any fertilizer. Your own faults, which for the time being you have not mastered and which you will never succeed

in overcoming, are your manure. Give yourself to carrying them diligently to the field of God's good pleasure in true surrender. Spread your fertilizer over the good earth, and without the slightest doubt, precious and sweet fruits will grow from it with humble surrender.[12]

Do you feel anxious, dry, powerless, or sad? "That very suspense and desolation", writes de Caussade, "are verses in the canticle of darkness. It is a joy that not a single syllable is left out, and it all ends in a 'Gloria Patri'; therefore we pursue the way of our wanderings, and darkness itself is a light for our guidance; and doubts are our best assurance. The more puzzled Isaac was to find something to sacrifice, the more completely did Abraham place all in the hands of Providence, and trust entirely in God."[13] "You continue to cling to your fears and doubts", he writes to a sister who complains to him. "You study them too much, instead of despising them and abandoning yourself entirely to God as I have preached to you for a long time past. Without this happy and holy abandonment you will never enjoy a solid peace."[14] Just as God's Providence is so all-encompassing that nothing falls outside of it and that even sin finds its proper place in it, so also, our surrender ought to be so perfect that even our worry, our troubles, and our temptations are enclosed in it and fall into place in it.

[12] *La Vie Spirituelle*, no. 652, p. 705.
[13] De Caussade, *Abandonment to Divine Providence*, p. 76.
[14] Ibid., Letters, p. 189.

Not even our troubles need to be a source of trouble. We cannot always live in total peace. "If God takes away your peace of mind, very well, let it go with the rest; God remains always, and when nothing else is left to you."[15]

Sometimes God can seem cruel. We can get the impression that it is *he* who is the great tormentor. But if he tries us, it is because his mercy never gives up. He continues to believe all things, hope all things, and try all things to get us to let go and surrender. Instead of thinking that God is impossible, we ought to be thankful that he never gets discouraged. God knows us. He knows how fixed we are on ourselves and how inclined to make our own ego the center, even in our love. He knows that if he lets us experience his sweet presence too soon or for too long, we will become so satisfied with our love for him that we will think more about that than about him. Yes, our nature is such that God's sweetness can make us forget God. God's love for us forces him to seem to withdraw, so that our self-love and pride will no longer have a stronghold. When self-love no longer receives any nourishment, in the end it can only starve to death. Only when self-love is dead and the center has moved from the individual to God can he communicate himself without any risk involved.

"As they go through the valley of Baca, they make it a place of springs" (Ps 84:6). Yes when one really accepts going "through the valley of Baca [tears]",

[15] Ibid., p. 363.

to be guided through it by him, it suddenly becomes evident that it is rich with springs. We do not need to wait until we have gone through the whole valley to see retrospectively that there were truly springs in abundance there. We discover them on the journey itself. That is one of the miracles of surrender. What appears as something monotonous and hopeless to an outsider and to one who stubbornly resists God's guidance becomes glorious to the one who trusts God and lets him decide. The child in us loves to walk in that way, with eyes closed, led by another with unconditional trust. Saint Thérèse of the Child Jesus tells how she enjoyed walking in that way, holding her father's hand and experiencing the security that lies in complete confidence in someone who is absolutely trustworthy. When seen in this way, an ordinary walk becomes an exciting adventure.

If we do not dare to walk hand in hand with God, whose hand shall we choose? Can God lead us astray? Can we trust more in our own limited vision than in him who has an overview of the whole journey? Is it not ridiculous to think that certain things could be lacking to us or that someone or something could put obstacles in our way? God knows exactly what we need. Everything he gives is carefully measured to our needs. He is the only one who knows our *true* needs. When we complain, we usually do it because of our *imaginary* needs.

The one who willingly lets himself be led by God walks on a very straight path. He saves an infinite amount of time and trouble. Most Christians invest a great deal of their energy in resisting God. As soon as we stop struggling, an unbelievable amount of energy is released. We suddenly move at a much quicker pace and are much happier. Resistance to life and its circumstances creates an inner cramp, which is the main and most significant reason for people's unhappiness. If this cramp disappears, everything becomes much easier. Then there is no longer any possibility of frustration. Frustration comes when we do not get what we think we need, when what we expect does not happen. Those who trust that God is guiding everything can never be frustrated. If they do not get a certain thing, they know they do not need it. If something they have waited for does not happen, they conclude that it is not meant for them. They are not disappointed, because everything is just as it should be; not in itself; far from it, but as the environment they are to live in, a "divine environment".

"For You, O Lord, Have Made Me Glad by Your Work" (Ps 92:4)

Those who live in this way are content with God. They think that he does everything very well. They have, of course, all they need, not too much and not too little. They willingly quote with Saint Thérèse the passage from Isaiah: "Tell the just man *all* is well" (3:10, from the Vulgate). "Yes, all is well when one seeks only the will of Jesus."[16] When God does everything so well, we can do nothing but congratulate him. "You have given me *delight*, O Lord, in *all* your doings."[17] These words should not be misunderstood as though it is easy to speak in this way when everything "goes well". Humanly speaking, it was not going well for Saint Thérèse at the time she wrote them. On the same page we read of her night of faith, which deprived her completely of the joy she had previously had in her faith.

In a person who is content with God and all that he does, there is an inner music, a song, which is sung of itself. The Carmelite nun Marie-Angélique of Jesus (1893–1919) from the monastery in Pontoise writes: "In my inmost being there is something that always sings, a Magnificat that never ceases." She does not call herself "flamme de joie" (flame of joy) for nothing. "One day", relates Monsieur Toccanier, who was chaplain with the holy Curé of Ars, "I said to him in passing: 'The weather is bad today, monsieur le Curé.' 'The weather is always beautiful for the just man,' he answered, 'it is only bad weather for poor sinners.' "[18]

---

[16] Thérèse of Lisieux, *Story of a Soul*, trans. John Clarke, O.C.D. (Washington D.C.: ICS Publications, 1976), p. 207.

[17] Ibid., p. 214.

[18] Francis Trochu, *Le Curé d'Ars* (Lyons-Paris: Vitte, 1929), p. 508.

Surrendering Our Past

God is present in all that happens, whether he directly wills it or permits it. Up to now we have mostly considered what this means for the present and the future. If we really believe that God's Providence embraces absolutely everything, we live in the *present* with an open and assenting attitude. Everything that happens is a message to us from God, which we receive and integrate into our lives. We look toward the *future* without worry, for we have only to walk in the good works prepared for us (Eph 2:10); everything is arranged by God.

But what about our past and the things we have still not really accepted; wounds that have not healed but, on the contrary, have become infected? Sometimes an unpleasant word from someone or an insignificant event in our lives brings forth a totally disproportionate reaction, which shocks not only those around us but even ourselves? Was it perhaps an old, unhealed wound that was laid bare? Or are we among those who can never be truly happy; people who have in their depths a permanent, diffuse sorrow, not because they are strangers on the earth who long for the heavenly city (Heb 11:13–16), but because of some unaccepted, repressed feelings that stifle their whole emotional life? We have not been able consciously to accept and assent to so much of what wounded us when we were small simply because God was still not real enough for us. Now we know that he was there, but we did not know it *then*. It seemed totally meaningless, and everything that is meaningless has a disastrous effect. Perhaps it is not enough that we understand now that God was there. That knowledge may be too theoretical, too abstract. Theories and abstractions have never helped anyone.

Those very traumatic events in our lives give us a privileged opportunity to let God's love become concrete for us. What the psychoanalyst strives to do by bringing traumatic experiences to consciousness often comes about much quicker and more completely by the action of the Holy Spirit. "The spirit of man is the lamp of the LORD, searching all his innermost parts" (Prov 20:27). We can ask him to illuminate our past and lead us to those incidents that we have still not accepted wholeheartedly. We can save a lot of time if we go into analysis with the Holy Spirit. An ordinary analysis normally takes many, many hours. If we only dedicated one-tenth of this time to contact with the Spirit, who is our true and ultimate therapist, in most cases we would progress much more quickly.

Nothing is hidden from him. ". . . my frame was not hidden from you, when I was being made in secret. . . . Your eyes beheld my unformed substance; in your book were written, every one of them, the days that were formed for me" (Ps 139:15–16). He

sees all and knows all. When we open ourselves to
him, we participate in his knowledge.

It is characteristic of the Spirit to place everything
in a larger context. He reveals that the Father was
present in all that you experienced in your life. What
looked so terrible and caused such pain was in *reality* not so bad. ". . . In all their affliction he was afflicted, and the angel of his presence saved them. . . .
He lifted them up and carried them all the days of
old" (Is 63:9). God carried you when you thought
that you were faltering; he surrounded you with his
love when you felt you were abandoned. The Spirit
helps you to see the whole of reality and not just a
small fragment. It is possible that you were not welcome when you were born into this cold world, but
God has welcomed you. "Before I formed you in
the womb I knew you" (Jer 1:5); ". . . borne by me
from your birth, carried from the womb" (Is 46:3).
Perhaps your mother did not have time for you when
you were small. Perhaps you felt abandoned by her.
Maybe you were harassed in school, or you are simply so sensitive and vulnerable that what is insignificant to others caused deep wounds in you. But now,
in the light of the Spirit, you understand that you
were never really left alone. "I have called you by
name, you are mine. When you pass through the waters I will be with you; and through the rivers, they
shall not overwhelm you; when you walk through
fire, you shall not be burned; the flame shall not

consume you. . . . Fear not, for I am with you" (Is 43:1-2, 5).

"I am with you." He can truly say this, for he has gone through all of it himself. He has experienced the indifference, hardness, and cruelty of mankind. He has suffered through all your anguish, loneliness, and despair. Everything that wounds you has wounded him first. He has freely taken all of it upon himself, so that you should never have to say that you are alone. You can never say to him: "You do not know what this is, you do not know what you are speaking about." Yes, he knows. He has already suffered everything. All fear, loneliness, and disappointment have been gathered together in him. It has received a positive stamp by the fact that he has gone through it. Every time a painful memory comes back, you can, so to speak, welcome it in Jesus' name. All your memories are also his memories, and your wounds are his wounds.

A New Past

We not only have the ability to form and shape our present and future, we also have power over our past. When we see our past in the light of the Holy Spirit, with the eyes of God, it is created anew. What we pray for in the Psalms comes true: "Make us glad as many days as you have afflicted us, and as many years as we have seen evil" (Ps 90:15). We receive a

completely new past. The best moment for this transformation of our past is, of course, at the Eucharist.
Do we really mean it when we say: "Say but the
word *and I shall be healed*?" He comes to us to heal
all wounds, to transform all sorrow into joy. Do we
give him the opportunity to heal us? Do we show
him our wounds? We pray: "In your wounds you
hide me."[19] "By his wounds you have been healed",
we read in the first letter of Peter (1 Pet 2:24). The
more we come in contact with these wounds, the
more all of our wounds heal. In the Eucharist, the
Lord comes to us wounded and sacrificed. That is the
right moment to pray: "Jesus, heal these wounds."

As soon as you show him your wounds and ex-
pose yourself to his healing power, the healing process begins, one that is not like ordinary healing. It
is not a question of something old that has caused
you much pain and finally ceases to torment you.
The healing goes back into time and transforms the
very moment when you were hurt into a moment
of grace. The very wound that was the cause of so
much suffering is transformed into a blessing, and all
the bitterness it caused is changed into meaningful
and fruitful suffering. When Israel could not drink
the water in Marah because of its bitterness, Moses
called out to the Lord: ". . . he cried to the LORD;
and the LORD showed him a tree, and he threw it into
the water, and the water became sweet" (Ex 15:23–

[19] Prayer, "Anima Christi".

25). The wood that we throw into the bitter water is the word "Amen": it is good as it is, and it was good even then, because you, O God, were there.

God was there. That is the very first and most important thing that our reading of the Scriptures can teach us: God is there in everything that happens. In the Bible we are dealing with the first cause, not the second. The most dramatic event in Joseph's life, when his brothers sold him, was God's greatest grace. "God sent me before you", he says to his brothers who came to Egypt to buy grain, "to preserve for you a remnant on earth, and to keep alive for you many survivors. So it was not you who sent me here, but God" (Gen 45:7–8). "You meant evil against me; but God meant it for good, to bring it about that many people should be kept alive, as they are today" (Gen 50:20).

A Healthy Memory

Gradually our whole memory becomes purified and healed. We can never overemphasize the significance of having a sound and healthy memory. The memory is often regarded as the least important of the three spiritual faculties (understanding, will, memory). For Augustine it was not so. He considers memory to be the very foundation from which the other two faculties are born. Thanks to memory, I can "remind" myself that I came from God and am related to him. It is memory that enables me to know myself as the same person from birth to death. It is thanks to memory that I know myself to be identical to the person I was ten years ago. My identity is dependent upon my memory. My whole life is stored in my memory.

What is it that fills our memory? Is it disappointments, failures, humiliations? Is our memory filled with bitterness? We understand Saint John of the Cross when he states that: ". . . All the great delusions and evils the devil produces in the soul enter through the ideas and discursive acts of the memory."[20] How can God work with us when we wake each morning with a heavy burden that we carry around day after day? Yet it is not necessary to live in this way. All those difficult and heavy things can be transformed and transfigured from within, so that they become positive memories filled with light. Instead of remembering disappointments and frustrations, we now remember how God came to meet us in our life.

> Pouring out a thousand graces,
> He passed these groves in haste,
> And having looked at them,
> With His image alone
> Clothed them in beauty.[21]

We remember his love that met us in everything, even in the most difficult moments. When Thérèse of Lisieux begins her autobiography, she thinks not so

[20] John of the Cross, *Ascent of Mount Carmel*, in *Collected Works*, p. 221.

[21] John of the Cross, *Spiritual Canticle*, stanza 5, in *Collected Works*, p. 434.

much of her life as of God's mercy, which was made manifest in her life. "I'm going to be doing only one thing: I shall begin to sing what I must sing eternally: 'The mercies of the Lord'" (les miséricordes du Seigneur).[22] A little farther on she writes:

> It is not, then, my life properly so called that I am going to write; it is my *thoughts* on the graces God deigned to grant me. I find myself at a period in my life when I can cast a glance upon the past; my soul has matured in the crucible of exterior and interior trials. And now, like a flower strengthened by the storm, I can raise my head and see the words of Psalm 22 realized in me: "The Lord is my Shepherd, I shall not want. . . ." To me the Lord has always been "merciful and good, slow to anger and abounding in steadfast love." (Ps 102:8)
>
> It is with great happiness, then, that I come to sing the mercies of the Lord with you, dear Mother.[23]

That is a healthy memory! A healthy memory does not mean that one forgets the difficult things of the past and remembers only happy events. No, a memory becomes healthy to the extent that it increasingly coincides with God's memory. We begin to see with his eyes and remember his work. We see that we are "the work of his hands". Our memory becomes healthy to the extent that we surrender our past to God and know that it is more his past than ours.

---

[22] Thérèse of Lisieux, *Story of a Soul*, p. 13.
[23] Ibid., p. 15.

2

Obeying God's Will

In the previous chapter we considered the first stage
of surrender: to accept and consent to God's will
as it is revealed to us in the circumstances of life.
We could call it the passive dimension of surrender,
as long as we do not confuse passivity with laziness
or laxity. Everyone who tries to say with Brother
Charles de Foucauld: "Whatever you do with me, I
thank you. I am ready for everything. I consent to
all", knows that this does not happen automatically
but, rather, demands an active and conscious decision
that can cost blood and tears. But since it has to do
with things that occur independently of our will and
that we cannot directly influence, it is enough to say
"yes, Father".

The second stage, however, consists of the aspect
of God's will that gives us something to *do* and that
comes with concrete tasks to be done. To say "yes,
Father" here means putting one's hand to the plow,
being God's obedient servant.

God's Obedience

When we speak of obedience, our thoughts ought to turn spontaneously and immediately to God. In the Holy Trinity there is a total and absolute obedience. The three Divine Persons are in perfect harmony with one another. None of them wants to do what is displeasing to the others. Rublev's famous icon expresses this absolute concord and harmony in an excellent way. There is no shadow of conflict in the Holy Trinity. Each one consents to the will of the other. The Father is the source of life. He wants to give of himself and beget a Son who is like him. The Son is willing to reflect the Father's being. He wants to be the Word of the Father and nothing else. "He who has seen me has seen the Father" (Jn 14:9). The Spirit is witness to this mutual love and desires to be nothing else.

This divine obedience becomes visible in Jesus. "My food is to do the will of him who sent me," he says, "and to accomplish his work" (Jn 4:34). "I can do nothing on my own authority . . . because I seek not my own will but the will of him who sent me" (Jn 5:30). "I have come down from heaven, not to do my own will, but the will of him who sent me" (Jn 6:38). "Truly, truly, I say to you, the Son can do nothing of his own accord, but only what he sees the Father doing; for whatever he does, that the Son does likewise" (Jn 5:19). In his farewell discourse at the end of his life, Jesus can testify: "I glorified you on earth, having accomplished the work which you gave me to do" (Jn 17:4). Even after his death Jesus is obedient. The Father raises him to life, and he lets himself be raised. His Ascension into heaven is a final act of obedience. In no way does he turn off his course. He goes the shortest and quickest way to the Father, and he takes up with him all whom the Father has given him. That includes us! "[He] raised us up with [Christ], and made us sit with him in the heavenly places in Christ Jesus" (Eph 2:6).

Jesus invites us to follow this path of obedience with him and in the same way he did. If we ask a mature Christian to speak about his journey to God, it will always be a story of obedience, though the word itself may not be mentioned. He has said Yes to God, and at certain times a more conscious, decisive, and perhaps dramatic Yes, which has borne fruit and led him to say Yes again and again. Without a Yes to God, nothing can mature in a person's life. If one's life is barren, the reason behind it is always the frequent repetition of the word No.

Jesus wants us, in him, to take part in the obedience and unity of the Trinity. Our Yes leads us into his Yes. "The Son of God, Jesus Christ, . . . was not Yes and No; but in him it is always Yes" (2 Cor 1:19). In and through him we may participate in that indescribable triune Yes that the Divine Persons say to one another.

Does God Will Something at Every Moment?

Perhaps the question will be more clear when I quote my former philosophy professor, who used to say that we do not need to look at the stars to find out what God wills, something he thought Christians had done all too often. "God's will is not written somewhere up in the heavens. Since God has given us a free will, he also wants us to use it. As long as we do not expressly violate God's revealed will and the laws of the Church, we can decide for ourselves what we want to do. If we act with sound reason, we are doing God's will. In some way we are the ones who decide what God's will is, and we are the ones who create it."

It sounds like an attractive idea, and we may be enthusiastic, but that does not prove the professor was right. I once asked a good friend if God wills something in everything, even in the smallest things. The answer came immediately: "Of course, otherwise obedience would have no meaning." In all its simplicity, it is a convincing answer. It is hardly conceivable that obedience should apply only to certain areas of our lives or certain times, even though many Christians may see it that way. A part of the day goes to "duty": work, a little time for prayer, and then during the remaining hours we do what we want; a time of obedience and a time of freedom. Can that be right? Is obedience not an attitude of life, something that influences and permeates one's whole existence? Adrienne von Speyr writes: "One cannot imagine that when Jesus decided to preach or pray, he did it with the feeling: 'I could just as well have done something else.'"[1] One might object that he had his own will and could choose for himself or that he wanted to do something for the Father and did it according to his own plans. But these objections are unfounded. What is decisive is Christ's untiring Yes, only that. Obedience means so much to him that he continually makes it a new expression of his love.

Can we imagine Mary dividing her life up into times of obedience and times of freedom? Was she not the handmaid of the Lord, living under the guidance of the Holy Spirit at every moment, from beginning to end? "Behold, as the eyes of servants look to the hand of their master, as the eyes of a maid to the hand of her mistress, so our eyes look to the LORD our God" (Ps 123:2). That is how Mary lived, with her eyes continually turned toward God. Her gaze was one single question: "What would you have me do?" "All who are led by the Spirit of God are sons of God", writes Saint Paul (Rom 8:14). Can we think that God's Spirit guides a person only now and then, when in fact it is the Spirit's life in us that characterizes the Christian life? Saint Paul points out clearly that this guidance of the Holy Spirit does not deprive us of our freedom. The text continues: "You did not receive the spirit of slavery" (Rom 8:15).

To content oneself with doing one's "daily duties"

---

[1] *Das Buch vom Gehorsam* (Einsiedeln: Johannes Verlag, 1966), pp. 101–2.

is an immature Christianity. Each moment comes with its own "duty" or, rather, its own task: an invitation from God to do something definite. De Caussade says one should be like a hand on a clock that is always moving and at every second takes up exactly the space it should occupy. There is not a moment in life when we can say: this is an instant God has forgotten, an empty moment.

De Caussade distinguishes between three types of duty: (1) What we must do because of the commands of God and the Church. (2) What God's Providence allows to happen and which we must accept (the first chapter treated of this). (3) All that the Holy Spirit inspires us to do. The last category should eventually fill our whole life.

God does will something at every moment, but there is no need to seek it up in the "heavens". It is nearer to us than that. "For this commandment which I command you this day is not too hard for you, neither is it far off. It is not in heaven, that you should say, 'Who will go up for us to heaven, and bring it to us, that we may hear it and do it?' Neither is it beyond the sea, that you should say, 'Who will go over the sea for us, and bring it to us, that we may hear it and do it?' But the word is very near you; it is in your mouth and in your heart; so that you can do it" (Deut 30:11–14).

We are blessed as Christians: we know what God wills. It is a privilege to know his will. He always wants the best for us, of course. "Happy are we, O Israel, for we know what is pleasing to God" (Bar

4:4). "He declares his word to Jacob, his statutes and ordinances to Israel. He has not dealt thus with any other nation; they do not know his ordinances. Praise the LORD!" (Ps 147:19–20). Or listen to Moses and with what enthusiasm he speaks about the great privilege of being able to hear God's voice and know what pleases him:

> For ask now of the days that are past, which were before you, since the day that God created man upon the earth, and ask from one end of heaven to the other, whether such a great thing as this has ever happened or was ever heard of. Did any people ever hear the voice of God speaking out of the midst of the fire, as you have heard, and still live? . . . Out of heaven he let you hear his voice, that he might discipline you; and on earth he let you see his great fire, and you heard his words out of the midst of the fire. (Deut 4:32–33, 36)

Yes, truly out of the fire. The Spirit is a fire within us. If we have never experienced or at least suspected that we have a fire in us, it will not surprise us that we do not hear his voice.

Try to Discern the Will of the Lord (Eph 5:17)

If God does will something in every detail of our life, it is up to us to "discern the will of the Lord". To be able to "obey", we must "listen".

God speaks to us from without and within. He speaks from without through the Bible, which is his word, and through the Church, which interprets and proclaims his word. The Church is the extension of the Incarnation and has received the guarantee from Jesus himself that he stands behind what she says. "He who hears you hears me, and he who rejects you rejects me, and he who rejects me rejects him who sent me" (Lk 10:16). We must give priority to the will of God that comes to us from without. If there is a conflict between what I feel within me to be God's will and what the Church proclaims to be God's will, I ought to prefer the latter. Certainly everyone must follow his conscience, but a *Christian* conscience lets itself be enlightened by the Bible and the Church. For a Christian, the Church is "Mater et Magistra"; he lets himself be reared and formed by her. God also speaks outwardly through circumstances (see first chapter) and our obvious daily duties.

Alongside of these clearly determined ways, however, there is an area where the paths are not marked out so clearly. Should you buy a TV or not, or, if you have a TV, should you watch today's programs or not? Neither the Bible nor the Church says anything about this. At times, circumstances can lead us in a certain direction and at other times in another. In such cases it is a question of listening to God, who speaks from within. We believe we have a Spirit dwelling within us who wants to guide us and is not indifferent to what we do. When we pray for light about a certain thing, he does not answer: "It's all the same, do as you want." He works in a definite and concrete way, not just generally by, for example, pointing out the command of love. He wants our action to bear fruit in order that the lamp may be set on a stand so that it shines for all in the house to see (Mt 5:15).

How do we know what God wills? We ought to "probe the heart and listen to the inspirations of this unction," writes de Caussade, "which interprets the will of God according to circumstances. The divine action, concealed though it is, reveals its designs, not through ideas, but intuitively (*par instincts*)."[2] Scholastic theology speaks of "potentia oboedientialis": a faculty that makes us capable of obeying. It lies deeper than all the other faculties of the soul. It is by means of this that we are open to God and in direct contact with him.[3] It is innate in human beings. Since God wills to reveal himself to all, he creates human beings so that they are capable of receiving this revelation. Even from birth there is a door within the human person that stands open toward heaven. It is unfortunate that all too often one is taught to close this door.

How does this faculty of obedience function? It responds to God's will by an inner attraction, an instinct, and an intuition. De Caussade readily speaks of "attraits non suspects", an inner attraction, which there is no reason to doubt. It does not require much

[2] Rev. Jean-Pierre de Caussade, S.J., *Abandonment to Divine Providence* (Exeter: Sidney Lee, Catholic Records Press, 1921), p. 79.

[3] Camille C. speaks of a "faculté d'ouverture à Dieu". See Henri Caffarel, *Camille C. ou l'emprise de Dieu* (Paris: Éd. du Feu Nouveau, 1982), p. 220.

self-knowledge to realize that every inner attraction does not come from God. The better one knows oneself and, most of all, the better one knows God, the easier it is to distinguish between what comes from one's own ego and what comes from the deeper level where God dwells. Since God is a "God of peace" (cf. 1 Cor 14:33), his will leads, as a rule, to a deeper peace. Our egoism leads, on the other hand, to disappointment and emptiness. There is a criterion that can help us recognize God. If we feel a deeper peace after responding to an inner prompting, we can believe that we have said Yes to God. We often know beforehand if a certain action will bring us peace or unrest. We begin to develop an ability to discern, which makes it all the easier to recognize God.

A typical example of an inner attraction that comes from God is the vocation to religious life or the priesthood. One often asks: "How can I know that I am called?" It is generally not by a voice from heaven that tells us what we must do, but rather by a growing inner certitude of a divine invitation; a certitude that is then confirmed by the peace one experiences when, after much rebellion and a long drawn-out struggle, which shows one understands the seriousness of the call, one finally surrenders to God.

Listening to the Spirit, who speaks from within, is something totally different from obeying certain rules or doing one's duty. We understand the difference best when we think of Jesus. He does not try to realize a detailed plan that he has in his pocket.

His love for his Father is so great that he does not turn his gaze away from him even for a moment. He continually looks at the Father in order to know what he should do. Here everything is characterized by love. He carries on an uninterrupted dialogue with the Father. The Father asks, "Will you?" and the Son answers, "Yes, Father." This is far from Kant's categorical imperative or the flat and mediocre morality to which Christianity is often reduced.

Many turn to God only when they must make an important or definitive choice in life. They approach God as a computer, so to speak, who gives answers to certain questions. "We cannot put our lives into God's hands," writes Martin Lönnebo, "demanding that his will be done in just one choice. That is wrong. Often we do not get a clear answer when we ask God questions in prayer. We can stand there just as perplexed after prayer as before. The secret of evangelical freedom from care is not that we surrender our life to God only at certain times. The secret is rather that we never leave God! Let your whole life rest in his powerful yet tender hand."[4]

"Who is the man that fears the LORD? Him will he instruct in the way he should choose" (Ps 25:12). If our sense of obedience has not developed by a continual assent to God's clear and certain will, we cannot count on being able to perceive his will when we find ourselves before a difficult and unclear choice.

---

[4] Söndagstankar, "Valet", *i Svenska Dagbladet*, January 16, 1983.

Openness and Availability

The condition for perceiving the impulses of the Holy
Spirit is a fundamental attitude of readiness and openness. We can learn this attitude from Mary. She would
never have been the Mother of the Lord if she had
not first been "the handmaid of the Lord". She does
not pose any unnecessary questions about which way
she should choose. She knows that his way is also her
way. "For a Christian who wishes to distinguish himself before God," writes Adrienne von Speyr, "there
is always the possibility of trying to do great things on
one's own, but that does not go very far. True growth
consists in placing oneself, without reserve, at the disposal of the Lord's will, which is still unknown. This
form of readiness is typically Catholic. It alone brings
about a complete openness. . . . Following the Lord's
example, a Catholic never chooses anything in particular. He chooses obedience and nothing more."[5]

In a commentary on the words of Saint Paul,
"Do you not know that your bodies are members
of Christ?" (1 Cor 6:15), she writes:

The fact that the Lord reigns over us and has us at
his disposal is not something merely theoretical that
is never or only rarely carried out. Nor is it some-

[5] Barbara Albrecht, *Eine Theologie des Katholischen: Einführung in
das Werk Adrienne von Speyrs*, vol. 1 (Einsiedeln: Johannes Verlag,
1972), p. 178.

thing limited; rather, it is something actual and absolute, which expresses itself by the demands of a total
obedience. He wants to be able to use us according
to his good pleasure with the same ease that a person
uses his limbs. We do not need to spend time weigh-
ing the pros and cons on every occasion to see if in
this case we will let ourselves be used or not, or how
long and to what extent, if the Lord really intends
to use us, or if someone else could not do him this
service. There is only an unconditional readiness, a
will to say Yes, an obedience, which, in fact, already
exists more in the Lord than in us. We ought to be
Christ's members to the degree that we receive his
impulses, just as bodily members understand the impulses of the human will and translate them into action. The Lord's desire to use us affects everything
in us. Not only what we know, but also everything
that is unknown to us.[6]

Yes, even what is unknown to us. God says to each
one of us: "You can do more than you realize." There
is so much that slumbers and waits to be awakened
within us. God also wants to use our unconscious
powers and possibilities. This explains the feeling of
Überforderung (excessive demands), which sooner or
later arises when we place ourselves at God's disposal.
We believe that we do not have the strength; that God
asks too much; but we have more than we think. We
have just enough strength as God wills. When he
gives a mission, he is obliged to give the strength

[6] Ibid., p. 180.

necessary to carry it out. If awakening the dormant powers is not enough, he creates new ones or does everything himself. This is what he does in the sacraments. What priest can say by his own power: "I absolve you from your sins"?

Detachment

Total readiness presupposes and includes detachment. Readiness and detachment are two sides of the same coin. Those who do not prefer one thing to another are detached. They are not drawn more to one thing than to another, or if they are, they do not pay attention to this attraction. They do not live in it. They want nothing but this: that God's will be done "on earth as it is in heaven". When they choose between two things, they do not choose one and reject the other. Such a choice is always a limitation and reduction: one decides against something else. Those who live in detachment never decide against anything. They choose, not a thing, but, rather, God's will.

Saint Thérèse's "I choose all" in all its childlikeness is not an inner contradiction.[7] For those who choose

---

[7] Thérèse relates how her sister Léonie came one day with a basket full of doll's clothes. She let Céline and Thérèse choose from among these treasures. Céline took a small bundle of wool. Thérèse, however, stretched out her hand and said: "I choose all" and took the whole basket without further ceremony. She adds that this little episode of her childhood summed up her whole life. See Thérèse of Lisieux, *Story of a Soul*, trans. John Clarke, O.C.D. (Washington D.C.: ICS Publications, 1976), p. 27.

God's will, nothing is ever lost. How could one lose anything by choosing God, who is everything (Sir 43:27)? It is our egotistic will, our natural partiality, that makes everything so small and narrow. As soon as we give up all of our own desires, we begin to have a share in the boundlessness of God. This is not something we know only by faith, but something we can clearly experience.

The closer we come to this detachment, the less we plan. How much of our planning is a waste of time! We plan very many things that never happen, and we must constantly change our plans. Those who are detached can wait; they have patience. God's will reveals itself at the proper time, not before. Martin Lönnebo speaks of "the importance of giving life time. For most of us, a hasty decision is not good, especially if it is based on a passing emotion or an intellectual analysis. The deepest decisions ought to be made with the whole body, and not the least in the heart."[8] It is in the heart that the Spirit lives and where we perceive his impulses. The Spirit has his plans, and when we have patience, he discloses them to us. There is perhaps no more effective way to die to oneself than by patience. The natural man wants to know what is going to happen. He wants to foresee, decide, and make plans. There is no limit to his impulsiveness. By not listening to him, but by listening patiently instead to what the Spirit is saying to our heart, the old man in us moves toward a certain death.

[8] See note 4, above.

We would misunderstand detachment completely if we thought that it turns one into a kind of puppet. God does not want people to obey like a machine. Each person has a personality with a distinct temperament and different strengths and gifts. All that we are and have must become a part of our service. We must love God with "all our strength". We are not instruments without a will that carry out his work mechanically. When God wants us to do a certain work, it becomes meaningful and dear to us. We ought to love it with the same love with which we love God. It requires a total surrender. God's will does not hover over the work, nor is it behind the work. God's will is in the work itself. Just as God's Word is incarnate, so also is his will.

Living in the Present

It is an inexhaustible source of wonder and admiration that God's will, which is so great and so far-reaching that it encompasses the whole universe, can make itself so small. Who does not think of the Eucharist here? We can meet God in nature, admire his power and majesty in the storm and his infinite greatness in the ocean, but we meet him much more in the small Host. There, in what appears to be only a little piece of bread, his whole presence is concentrated. It is the same with God's will. I can speculate with Teilhard de Chardin about God's will for the world and humanity, about development toward the omega point, but I live much *more* in God's will when I do the little, ordinary work he gives me to do right now. Yes, the more consciously I live and the more concentrated I am in the moment, the more I am one with God's will. It is in the very smallest things that I meet the very greatest.

Every person comes into the world with a dream of doing something great with his life, something that will make an imprint and bear fruit. God himself inspires this dream. He is, of course, the one who makes the human person great. "You have made him little less than the angels, and you have crowned him with glory and honor" (Ps 8:6). If only we could understand that we can only realize our dream by being totally present to the little and insignificant things we have to do at each moment. We encounter the infinity of God only in the present moment. The more we are recollected in the moment, the more clearly does the eternal now of God reveal itself.

The infinity of God comes to us through a funnel. It becomes so little and so narrow that it is difficult for us to recognize it. It comes only drop by drop through the small opening. The funnel is the present moment. When I put my mouth to the funnel, I am nourished by infinity. Even this is something we can experience. The more concentrated we are and the more we live from moment to moment, the more space opens up to us and we feel we are living in a kind of boundlessness. The present moment is the incarnation of God's eternity. Those who live in the present moment drink unceasingly of eternity.

"In the state of abandonment," writes de Caussade,

the only rule is the duty of the present moment. In
this the soul is light as a feather, liquid as water, sim-
ple as a child, active as a ball in receiving and following all the inspirations of grace. Such souls have
no more consistence and rigidity than molten metal.
As this takes any form according to the mould into
which it is poured, so these souls are pliant and easily receptive of any form that God chooses to give
them. In a word, their disposition resembles the at-
mosphere, which is affected by every breeze; or water, which flows into any shaped vessel exactly filling
every crevice.[9]

There is a tremendous flexibility and mobility in
those who increasingly strive to live in the present
moment. They are completely synchronized with
God. We ordinarily get stuck in what was once God's
will but is no longer, or we already live in what will
probably be God's will but often does not come to be.
Experience shows that we are always making wrong
prognoses. We often live in the past and the future
at the same time, which gives us a feeling of inner
division and is perhaps the main cause of our weari-
ness. We have not surrendered our past with its guilt
and painful wounds. We carry it with us like a heavy
burden. Nor do we dare to surrender our future to
God. We are afraid that he will take advantage of our
trust. How many there are who do not dare to pray:

[9] De Caussade, *Abandonment to Divine Providence*, p. 58.

"Do with me as you will. Whatever you do with me, I thank you. I am ready for everything. I consent to all. May only your will be done with me and with all you have created!" They nevertheless pray many times a day: "Your will be done on earth as it is in heaven."

When we are so preoccupied with our past and our future, we naturally have neither energy nor openness left for the present moment, the only moment that mediates God's will. Just as we usually sidestep our true personality, which is "light in the Lord" (Eph 5:8), we also usually seek God's will by the wayside, in the wrong place. We always come too early or too late and never hit upon the present moment. We are obstinate in wanting to eat something other than what God serves, and then we are surprised that we have indigestion! We prefer to eat either old leftovers or food that is not fully cooked, and we think it is strange that we do not feel well.

If, on the other hand, we try to be synchronized with God, we experience a well-being in both body and soul; an elasticity develops. Living in the present is actually an invaluable exercise. We work and cease to work, we read and put the book down again, we speak and are silent, eat and sleep, always totally present, but in a constantly changing environment. We never do two things at once, always one thing *after* the other. We turn in different directions as the present moment, which is God's ambassador, invites us. We are like Saint John of the Cross' solitary bird, which turns its beak toward the wind, that is, toward the Holy Spirit.[10] "The wind [Spirit = *pneuma*, in Greek] blows where it wills," says Jesus, "and you hear the sound of it, but you do not know where it comes from or where it goes" (Jn 3:8). We do not need to know. The only thing that matters is to be docile. The best remedy for the spiritual rheumatism from which most of us suffer is this continual exercise. Our reactions are impeded and slow because we cling to old experiences and behavioral patterns.

When we are fully synchronized with God, we never lose out on anything. We receive exactly what he wants to give us, and always in full measure. At the same time, we receive a minimum of unnecessary troubles and fruitless suffering. "How is your fever", writes Jesuit Father August Valensin to François, "confounded in its future existence, of which we do not yet know if our Father wills it, but blessed and welcomed as his messenger in its present existence? There is no contradiction between this hatred and this love, this rejection and this acceptance. When the event *is*, it is always a bearer of grace. Before it is, it is only itself—often something terrible. This is one of the secrets of joy."[11]

[10] John of the Cross, "Maxims on Love", no. 42, in *The Collected Works of Saint John of the Cross* (Washington, D.C.: I.C.S. Publications, 1979), p. 677.

[11] Auguste Valensin, *Francois* (Paris: Aubier-Montaigne, 1964), p. 282.

Boundlessness and Unity

Those who do their own will are constantly run-
ning into their own limitations. Everything is cen-
tered on them and bears the stamp of it. As long as
the ego makes decisions autonomously, all that happens is ego-centered and marked by the limitations of
the ego. But the more a person begins to obey, the
more his ego disappears, enabling him to do God's
will. God's will knows no boundaries. He wants to
be everything, everywhere (1 Cor 15:28). To live in
his will is to live without borders, to share in his
boundlessness. As a result, one's life reflects an inner
harmony and unity.

I spoke of an elasticity and flexibility that make a
person capable of a multitude of constantly changing tasks. But this multitude does not exclude unity
(just as the "trinity" in God does not exclude his
unity). Those who obey God's will always do essen-
tially the same thing. It is the will of God that gives
things their substantial reality. In itself everything is
created as "vanity of vanities" (Eccles 1:2). Even Saint
Teresa of Avila says: "everything is nothing" (no era
todo nada). But as soon as something comes into the
magnetic field of God's will, its emptiness is filled.
It is the same electrical current that flows through
all that comes in contact with God's will. In themselves, objects are like the dry bones that we read
about in Ezekiel, but when God's Spirit comes into

them, they become living human beings (Ezek 37:1–
14). Father de Caussade speaks about a double "reduction". (1) First everything is reduced to nothing:
"When everything created in this way dissolves into
nothing . . .", or, with Saint Paul's words, "For his
sake I have suffered the loss of all things, and count
them as refuse, in order that I may gain Christ" (Phil
3:8). (2) Everything submits "to the order of God".
What I have to do at each moment and what in itself
belongs to this "nothing" is suddenly given a new
value by God's will. His will makes what was dead
rise up again.[12]

Since it is God's will alone that gives things their
reality, the one who obeys God always does the
same thing. It is only on the surface that occupations
change. "A contemplative person", writes Chapman
(1865–1933), (I would like to translate: a person who
lives in complete surrender to God's will),

> does the same thing night and day. He prays, eats
> breakfast, works, speaks or relaxes, but he knows,
> above all, that he is doing God's will. The different
> occupations seem to him to be the visible manifesta-
> tions of an abiding inner disposition.
>
> Think of a long walk; one goes up the hill and
> down the hill, in rain, sun or wind, but the action of
> walking is always the same, the same leg movement;
> now light, now heavy, now pleasant, now unpleas-
> ant.[13]

[12] De Caussade, *Abandonment to Divine Providence*, p. 52.
[13] Dom Chapman, *Spiritual Letters* (London: Sheed and Ward,
1969), p. 38.

Instead of coming in contact with different things, we now encounter God at all times. We get attached, not to the things, but to the hand of God that places them before us to make use of them. Instead of using things, we enjoy God's action and rejoice in it. It is he who gives us his gifts through these things.

In the beginning I spoke of the feeling of inner division we may feel when we try to keep all the rules and regulations that are part of the Christian ethic. This division becomes even worse when we begin to make different rules *ourselves*.

> As long as we are attached to a multitude of practices and rules formed by our own will [writes Tauler], as long as we are clothed in them, the Bridegroom cannot clothe us as he wills. Do not concern yourself with practices and works, but rather keep your whole attention turned toward God's will. Do not follow the one or the other. To do so is complete bondage. Do not look at people and how they behave: "O Lord, how I would like to be able to control myself! How I long to have inner peace and be like this or that person!" What is life for one is death for another. That is why you ought to consider, above all, the call God has given you and follow it. If you do it with great attentiveness, your vocation will seem to be as plain to you as your hand.[14]

---

[14] See Sr. Suzanne-Dominique, "L'Abandon, itinéraire spirituel d' après Tauler", in *La Vie Spirituelle*, no. 652, p. 699.

True Freedom

We might imagine that life becomes extremely tedious when we are always bound to God's will, particularly when that will extends to all the details of life. Never again to be able to do what we want! But listening to God and obeying him is precisely what we want. This becomes clearer if we distinguish between a superficial and a deep will in the human person. We often identify a person's will with what is merely his superficial will. The superficial will is usually at the service of egoism. It listens to all its conflicting impulses and lets itself be led by the notorious couple: "I like—I don't like." It also obeys reason, to the extent that it egotistically seeks profit and gain. The deep will, on the other hand, is at the service of love; it coincides with our innate desire for God. The deep will "wants" God, moves toward him, and finds its satisfaction in him.

When the superficial will is allowed to express itself and do what it wants, one can certainly get the impression of being free. But this freedom shares in the superficiality of the will and should in reality be called "slavery", since it stifles the deep freedom. The superficial and the deep will struggle against each other. "The desires of the flesh are against the Spirit, and the desires of the Spirit are against the flesh; for these are opposed to each other" (Gal 5:17). We realize we have become free only when we strive to live on the level of our deep will, and we discover how much we would lose if we continued living on the level of our superficial will.

Thus freedom and obedience are not opposed to each other. Freedom is genuine when it enables us to listen to God and assent to his will. "Freedom is that state in which the heart is no longer attached to anything, but can follow God's will" (Saint Francis de Sales). Freedom is finally being able to do what we were created for, to be united with our true nature and take root there. It is a question of being or not being. "To be or not to be, that is the question." If you are created as a stream toward God, be a stream. If you are created as an ear ("you have given me an open ear" [Ps 40:6]), be an ear. Being something other than what you are naturally leads away from freedom to a kind of schizophrenia. Saint Paul loves to speak about the freedom that Christ won for us, the freedom that consists in being slaves of God (Rom 6:22).

There is a wonderful harmony that exists between a person's true freedom and God's freedom. Those who are free (unfettered) give God the freedom to do what he wills. When you are free of all inhibitions and impediments, God is also free to fill you as he wills. What he has waited for so long can finally become reality. When all the threads that bind you to things are clipped, God can lead you to the goal at his own divine pace. Or, to use Saint John of the Cross' image: When all the windows and curtains are opened, the sunlight streams into the room of the

heart and completely illuminates it.[15] Light seeks to
shine; fire seeks to give warmth. Our freedom gives
God freedom.

If, thanks to a person's freedom, God is free to do
with him as he wills, surprising things happen all the
time. What God does is always new and original. "It
is the action", writes de Caussade,

> applied at each moment to produce ever new effects,
> and it will extend from eternity to eternity. It has pro-
> duced Abel, Noah, Abraham, all different types; Isaac,
> also original, and Jacob from no copy; neither does
> Joseph follow any prefigure. Moses has no prototype
> among his progenitors. David and the Prophets are
> quite apart from the Patriarchs. Saint John the Baptist
> stands alone. Jesus Christ is the first-born; the Apos-
> tles act more by the guidance of His spirit than in
> imitation of His works.
>
> Jesus Christ did not set a limit for Himself, neither
> did He follow all His own maxims to the letter. The
> Holy Spirit ever inspired His holy soul, and, being en-
> tirely abandoned to its every breath, it had no need
> to consult the moment that had passed, to know how
> to act in that which was coming. The breath of grace
> shaped every moment according to the eternal truths
> subsisting in the invisible and unfathomable wisdom
> of the Blessed Trinity. The saints receive a share in
> this divine life, and in each, Jesus Christ is different,
> although the same in Himself. The life of each saint is
> the life of Jesus Christ; it is a new gospel. The cheeks

[15] John of the Cross, *Living Flame of Love*, III, 46, in *Collected
Works*, p. 627.

of the spouse are compared to beds of flowers, to gardens filled with fragrant blossoms. The divine action is the gardener, admirably arranging the flowerbeds. This garden resembles no other, for among all the flowers there are no two alike, or that can be described as being of the same species, except in the fidelity with which they respond to the action of the Creator.[16]

God does not need to look for extraordinary tasks in order to make each person a unique being. It is by fulfilling the most ordinary duties that a person is original. Everyone who honestly tries to live in obedience to the Spirit's inspiration knows that a life that from the outside looks monotonous and dull can be very adventurous and exciting. It is the same with a person's external appearance. Every face has two eyes, two ears, a nose, and a mouth. Is there anything more monotonous than that? And yet what endless variation! There is a variation so great that we find it strange when two people "resemble" each other.

Then we understand that it can be risky to read the lives of saints *if* we do it with the intention of imitating them in every detail. What the life of a saint can inspire in us is the will to live in the same total obedience and surrender, in the same openness to the Spirit's constantly new impulses. It is fascinating to see what God can do with a person who is willing to

---

[16] De Caussade, *Abandonment to Divine Providence*, p. 60.

follow the Lamb wherever he goes (Rev 14:4). But it is good to know that the Lamb is totally "unpre-dictable" and that there is a new, surprising path for each person.

Mankind's Rebellion

Since the first sin of Adam in paradise, obedience is no longer self-evident. In practice we might say that disobedience has become the norm. If you want to be obedient, you have to overcome many obstacles, and each time you are disobedient, it is more difficult to be obedient the next time. Little by little, disobe-dience can become a fundamental attitude, affecting not only the will, but also the intellect. One begins to discuss with God and interrogate him. Discussion with God is as old as mankind. It began in paradise during the conversation between the woman and the serpent: Why should we not be allowed to eat of the fruit? Why this prohibition? If God takes our salva-tion seriously, why does he not reveal himself more clearly? Why does he make things so difficult for us? Why so much suffering? Why such unrealistic de-mands that no one can live up to? And finally, the fundamental question: Why did God make man ca-pable of sinning? Why did he not create him in a celestial state, so that sin was excluded? The Bible says: God saw that what he had made was good. But is it honest to say that everything was good? Should we not rather say that all of it was wrong from the beginning? Why did God create man so weak and foolish that sin was almost inevitable?

We could answer that God also created angels, who are neither weak nor foolish, and some of them, nevertheless, sinned. But this does not solve the whole problem. The answer to the question lies, paradoxically enough, in God's own love.[17]

God created mankind out of generosity. He wants, not to keep his life to himself, but rather for other beings to share in his abundance. That is why he created man "in his own image" (Gen 1:27). He wanted man to be like himself to the degree that that is possible. But who is God, and what is he like? He is self-gift. In the Holy Trinity, the Father gives himself completely to the Son. He does not say "I" but "you". To give himself is characteristic of his being; yes, this is the very heart of the matter. If God had created us in a celestial state from the beginning, so that we beheld him face to face, we would surely never have sinned, but something important would have been missing. We would not be able to share in the mutual giving, which is the essence of the Trinity. Our desire to give ourselves would never be satisfied, since we would see clearly that we gave nothing, that it was God who gave everything, even our love for him. We would see that we were carried away by the waves of love, borne on an irresistible current, without even being

---

[17] I summarize a few pages (80–85) out of M.-D. Molinié, O.P., *Prisonniers de l'Infini* (Paris: Cerf, 1977).

able to say a personal Yes to it. Life in heaven would have something unavoidable and irresistible about it. Each of us would be obliged to say: we have only received, and we have never given anything.

If we are subject to trials here on earth, if we must struggle to say Yes to God, it is because in eternity God wants to say to us: "You have given me something. It is not only I who give, but rather we give to each other. I give myself in gratitude because you have given me something that you could have refused to give. Now you can no longer give me anything, but at one time you did, and it has an eternal value. I never forget."

Theology has always taught that we cannot "merit" anything, either in heaven or in purgatory. To "merit", that is, to do something for God, belongs to our earthly life. In heaven one is like a straw that is carried by the ocean. There is love, an overflowing stream of love, but no voluntary giving. One is taken, filled, in ecstasy, but one does not actually "give", or, better said, one gives because one has once given, once freely said Yes to God, and now is fixed in that Yes forever.

We would have to be God to be able to give ourselves totally, in absolute freedom, without any possibility of saying No. Freedom and necessity coincide perfectly in him. To give is his nature, a nature that he has not received but that is. He is his own foundation. That is why self-giving in him is both inevitable and free. It is necessary for us to have an imperfect freedom so that we can give. If we want to be able to say Yes to God, we must also be able to say No. If it is not possible to say No, with all the sin and suffering it entails, if our Yes is inevitable, we cannot say that we give anything to God. A compulsory Yes would in itself be a gift from him and not, as it is with God, something we have of ourselves. And if we cannot give anything to God, we do not have a share in his Spirit, who by his very nature is Gift.

It is an essential element in our faith that human beings can give something to God, that, as Catholic theologians express it, we have "merit". Without this, we do not participate fully in the life of the Trinity, which consists of a mutual giving and receiving.

If God had let us behold his face from the beginning, we would have been fixed in a definitive state of mere receiving. But he wanted us to be like him and live in both giving and receiving.

He could not have shown us a greater honor!

3

Being God's Instrument

The first two stages of surrender can be summed up in submitting to God's will as it manifests itself in the various circumstances of life and obediently carrying out what he gives us to do. These two stages run somewhat parallel. We can call them the passive and active dimensions of surrender. The third stage, however, is completely new and presupposes that we have practiced accepting and obeying God's will for a long time. Here there is no longer any distinction between activity and passivity. Instead, we could speak of passive activity; the person is led by God in all his actions. In the third stage, we surrender ourselves and our faculties so completely to God that he is able to use them as he wills. In the second stage, it is I who do God's will, *I do it for him*. In the third stage, on the other hand, it is he who uses me; *he does it through me*.

This is something new, where different rules apply. "There is a time when the soul lives in God", writes de Caussade, "and a time when God lives in the soul."[1] It is a question of two different phases

---

[1] Rev. Jean-Pierre de Caussade, S.J., *Abandonment to Divine Providence* (Exeter: Sidney Lee, Catholic Records Press, 1921), p. 36.

that have their own characteristics. "When the soul lives in God it is obliged to procure for itself, carefully and very regularly, every means it can devise by which to arrive at the divine union. The procedure is marked out; the readings, the examinations, the resolutions. The guide is always at hand and everything is by rule, even the hours for conversation."[2] Here it is the person himself who decides and plans. He does it according to the old and tried ascetical rules. All of this is good and necessary during the first part of the journey, but it is completely different when God lives in the soul. "When God lives in the soul," continues de Caussade,

> it has nothing left of self, but only that which the spirit which actuates it imparts to it at each moment. Nothing is provided for the future, no road is marked out, but it is like a child which can be led wherever one pleases. . . . God, who finds no purer disposition in His spouse than this entire self-renunciation for the sake of living the life of grace according to the divine operation, provides her with necessary books, thoughts, insight into her own soul, advice and counsel, and the examples of the wise. Everything that others discover with great difficulty this soul finds in abandonment, and what they guard with care in order to be able to find it again, this soul receives at the moment there is occasion for it and afterward relinquishes so as to admit nothing but exactly what God desires it to have in order to live by Him alone.[3]

[2] Ibid.
[3] Ibid.

It is important not to practice this total dependency too soon. In order to surrender ourselves totally to God, we must first gather together all that we are and have. If we experience ourselves as a collection of scattered pieces, which we do not know how to fit together, there can be no question of total surrender. One cannot give oneself if he is no one. There must first be order created in one's being. What was scattered and lying about must be gathered and joined together to make a whole, or, in the language of Saint John of the Cross: One can only leave one's house when it has been "stilled".[4] Those who are accustomed to following their own tastes and desires[5] and who have still not learned to direct the four passions, joy, hope, sorrow, and fear, toward God[6] are not mature enough for this total dependency. But it is just as important, when the time is ripe, to dare to let go and surrender the helm to God. It is unfortunate that we obstinately persist in *walking*, when we are called to *fly* with the "speed of the Trinity" (P. Molinié). And often out of fear of false mysticism, we do not dare to speak about this other part of the journey, when we no longer have any right to decide for ourselves, when it is no longer I who live but Christ who lives in me (Gal 2:20), when it is really true that

[4] John of the Cross, *Dark Night of the Soul*, strophe 1, in *The Collected Works of Saint John of the Cross* (Washington, D.C.: I.C.S. Publications, 1979), p. 297.

[5] John of the Cross, *Spiritual Canticle*, strophe 20, 5, in *Collected Works*, p. 489.

[6] Ibid., 3, p. 489.

we "live by the Spirit" (Gal 5:25). There ought to come a time, in the life of every Christian, when he is merely God's instrument and nothing more.

Surrendering EVERYTHING

In the third stage, surrender is much more radical and "total" than in the second. There I refrained from choosing for myself what I would do. I tried to discover God's will and then carry it out, but it was *I* who did God's will. Now I offer to God not only my will but also all of my potential, all of the powers of my soul, so that *he* himself may carry out his will *through me*. Before, it was I who played the violin. It was God, of course, who gave me the score, and I obediently played what he gave me to play. Now I give the violin to God and let him play. One hears that it is the same violin. It has the same characteristics and defects. But there is no similarity between the music I produced myself and what resonates now. God not only makes use of all of the violin's possibilities, but he reveals something of himself in his playing. It is not that I have become more skilled. No, now an artist of the very highest grade is playing.

Being God's violin is something completely different from playing the violin for God. Now he does not content himself with deciding what I should play, but he himself touches the strings of my faculties. He can do that only when he has the violin in his hands, when my surrender applies, not just to one part of myself, but to my whole self. "I abandon myself into

Your hands", prays Brother Charles de Foucauld, "I offer it to You with all the love of my heart . . . and so need to give myself, to surrender myself into Your hands without reserve."

One does what God does and has always done: The Father gives his whole life to the Son, the Son gives it back to the Father, and the Spirit is himself this life that is given and poured out. To give one's life is to die. For many, death is the moment when life is taken away from them, the moment when God, who himself wants to be our life, finally conquers the insubordinate person and deprives him of that life which in his greed he seized and made his own, though it was and should have remained God's. As a rule, God must use a little force, because man resists right up to the end. Why wait so long with what must happen anyway and which becomes tremendously richer when it is done willingly? Why not say with Jesus: "No one takes [my life] from me, but I lay it down of my own accord" (Jn 10:18)?

There is another well-known prayer in Christian tradition that expresses this total surrender, namely, Ignatius of Loyola's "Suscipe": "Take, Lord, receive all my liberty, my memory, understanding, my entire will, all that I own and have. You have given it to me; to you, Lord, I return it. All is yours. Dispose of it wholly according to your will." It sounds wonderful, but we must admit that it is not easy to surrender oneself wholly to God. "It is just as easy", writes Chapman, "to cast oneself into an invisible fire, and it has the same effect. First it burns your clothing,

then your flesh and finally your bones. 'It is a terrible thing to fall into the hands of the living God'
(Heb 10:31). But he is infinite wisdom and love anyway. The question is, if the wide way is really more
comfortable than the narrow gate."[7] Yes, even if it is
difficult to surrender oneself to God, it is still more
difficult to struggle against him and resist him.

Can one love without surrendering oneself? True
love inevitably leads to total surrender. "To love is
to give everything and to give oneself", writes Saint
Thérèse of Lisieux, in her poem about Mary.[8] That is
why surrender is not optional. It is as binding as love.
"Love the Lord your God with all your strength"
means: "Surrender yourself totally." Those who do
not want the latter do not want the former.

"I have often noticed", writes the French mystic
Lucie Christine (1870–1908), "that an act of total
and absolute surrender to God's holy will almost always immediately brings about the grace of union."[9]
Perhaps we could even say that total surrender in itself *is* union. God says that when a man gives himself to his wife, they become one flesh (Gen 2:24).
He presupposes that the wife also gives herself to her
husband, but this mutuality is not a given in human
love. It is a given, however, when it comes to a rela-

[7] Dom Chapman, *Spiritual Letters* (London: Sheed and Ward,
1969), p. 62.

[8] "Pourquoi je t'aime, O Marie", strophe 22.

[9] *Journal Spirituel de Lucie Christine*, ed. Aug. Poulain (Paris:
Beauchesne, 1920), p. 52.

tionship with God. Surrender is total on his part. He *is* "body given" and "blood outpoured". He waits only for us to give ourselves. If we do so, union becomes a fact. He comes to us offered and completely surrendered to us in the Eucharist, in order to call forth the same surrender in us. If we do not receive the Eucharist with at least a desire for complete surrender, the whole thing becomes a lie. We hinder God when we do not want to respond to his total surrender with our total surrender.

Let God Act

The total surrender referred to here implies that we lay the entire responsibility upon God. We give him our understanding so that he will use it to think what he wills. We give him our will for his divine will to be incarnated, so that he may will through our human will. We give him our memory for him to touch it and make it remember what he considers important. We place ourselves and all of our powers at his disposal. We say to God: "You can bear the responsibility now", and he is happy, because this is what he has desired all along. Saint Teresa of Avila describes the final union with Christ in these words: "The Lord represented himself to her, just after she had received Communion, in the form of shining splendor, beauty, and majesty, as He was after His resurrection, and told her that now it was time that she consider as her own what belonged to Him and that

He would take care of what was hers."[10] God wants to take our concerns upon himself. It is true that this only becomes a definitive reality in the seventh mansion of the interior castle, but even now he wants us, as often as possible, to let him take over. If we do not do this, we will never reach the seventh mansion. This training, however, does not require any *effort* in the true sense of the word. In Paul Claudel's drama *The Satin Shoe*, the Jesuit father says: "One speaks of sacrifice, when in every choice that must be made it is only a question of an almost imperceptible movement, as that of a hand! In reality it is only evil that requires effort, since it struggles against reality." Fighting against reality is arduous; accepting reality always results in relief and liberation.

Father de Caussade speaks of "finding the divine impulse" (trouver la motion divine).[11] It is a question of pressing the right button, being on God's wavelength. In practice, it means that one lets go of one's own ego, that autonomous creature which wants to decide and act on its own. The ego is a cramp; therefore we do not get rid of it by exerting ourselves, but by relaxing. We let go, again and again. Not I, but you. Less and less I, more and more you, according to the golden rule formulated once and for all by the

[10] Teresa of Avila, *Interior Castle*, Collected Works of Saint Teresa of Avila, vol. 2 (Washington D.C.: ICS Publications, Institute of Carmelite Studies, 1980), p. 432.

[11] Jean-Pierre de Caussade, *L'Abandon à la providence divine* (Paris: Desclée de Brouwer, 1966), p. 122.

greatest of prophets: "He must increase, but I must decrease" (Jn 3:30).

God wants to be the life of man. He desires to be the principal agent in our actions. Father de Caussade uses a very expressive image: "In this state God communicates Himself to the soul as its life, but He is no longer visible as its way, and its truth. The bride seeks the Bridegroom during this night; she seeks Him before her, and hurries forward; but He is behind her, and holding her with His hands. He is no longer object, or idea, but principle and source."[12] Previously God's will was an object that was before us; it illumined the path: "Your word is a lamp to my feet and a light to my path" (Ps 119:105).

But there comes a time when God's will moves from the front to the back, resulting in the disappearance of the light. I can no longer see where I am going. God is behind me, and I have only one thing to do: Let myself be pushed along. In the beginning it feels a little uncertain and unsafe, and small accidents can occur, not because God fails to do his part or is leading in the wrong direction, but because I have not dared to trust in him completely, and I resist or want to help. God is like a specialist in relaxation who works with the patient's head, turning it in different directions. The fact that it causes pain is not the specialist's fault. He does not turn it too far. No, it is because the patient's neck muscles are tense. He

[12] De Caussade, *Abandonment to Divine Providence*, p. 75.

cannot, dares not relax completely. It is no wonder
God calls us a "stubborn people" (Deut 9:13).

The words "your kingdom come" that we pray
daily are realized only when we live in total depen-
dence on God. As long as he cannot do *everything* in
us, his kingdom has not come. He wants not merely
to decide himself; he also wants to carry out what he
has decided, "as though without me and yet through
me".[13] Our ego lives, thanks to and through our ac-
tivities. When we surrender our faculties to God and
let him manage them, the ego has nothing more to
do; it dies from lack of work.

In his advice to the novices, Eckhart writes: "God
has never given himself and does never give himself
to a will that is foreign to him. He gives himself only
to his own will. But *when* God meets his own will,
he gives himself and enters into that will with all that
he is."[14]

In the traditional language of theologians: in this
state, a person's life is regulated, no longer by the
virtues, but by the gifts of the Holy Spirit. At Bap-
tism, we receive, along with sanctifying grace, the
virtues (and above all the theological virtues: faith,
hope, and charity), and the gifts of the Holy Spirit.
These gifts of the Spirit give us a certain docility and
sensitivity to the guidance of the Spirit. They are
like antennas designed to pick up the impulses of the

[13] Jean de Saint-Samson (1571–1636).
[14] No. 21, see *La Vie Spirituelle*, no. 652, p. 773.

Holy Spirit. The difference between the virtues and the gifts is that, among other things, we can practice the virtues when and how we will. We can take the initiative ourselves in making an act of faith. But it is the Holy Spirit who activates the gifts. Therefore, what is produced by the gifts is more divine than human. We are completely passive in this state. The only thing we need to do is say Yes to God. "Magis agimur quam agimus", says Thomas Aquinas. "We become more acted upon than we act ourselves." These gifts of the Spirit are necessary for us to be able to live as children of God, for according to Saint Paul, God's children are those who are led by the Spirit of God (Rom 8:14). The fact that the Spirit takes the initiative does not mean that we can act divinely now and then and on certain occasions. The Spirit is prepared to lead us at *all times*. The question is: Are we prepared to *let ourselves be led?*

Saint John of the Cross' View

Saint John of the Cross speaks in detail about the third stage of surrender, when he treats of the night of memory.[15] He stresses that one should not let oneself be led by the knowledge of the memory. He quotes Jesus' words: "No one can serve two masters" (Mt 6:24). Either we lead ourselves and act independently,

---

[15] John of the Cross, *Ascent of Mount Carmel*, III, 1–15, in *Collected Works*, pp. 213–35.

or God is allowed to be Lord and we let ourselves be led by him.[16] What he says about the memory is only the application of a general principle:

> All these sensory means and exercises of the faculties must, consequently, be left behind and in silence so that God Himself may effect the divine union in the soul. As a result one has to follow this method of disencumbering, emptying, and depriving the faculties of their natural rights and operations to make room for the inflow and illumination of the supernatural. If a person does not turn his eyes from his natural capacity, he will not attain to so lofty a communication; rather he will hinder it.[17]

He speaks of a baldheaded memory (calva y rasa). Even Tauler (ca. 1300–1361) indicates that one should become a barber, not to shave others, but to shave oneself. All the hair, that is, all the inordinate desires, the little as well as the great, must be ruthlessly shaved off.[18] But John of the Cross wields the razor in a way that is even more radical. Not only inordinate desires are to be shaved off, but even the ordinary knowledge of the memory. "All these sensory means and exercises of the faculties must, consequently, be left behind. . . . As a result one has to follow this method of disencumbering, emptying and depriving the faculties of their natural rights and operations. . . . The

---

[16] Ibid., 2, 4, p. 215.
[17] Ibid., 2, 2, pp. 214–15.
[18] See *La Vie Spirituelle*, no. 652, p. 700.

annihilation of the memory in regard to all forms is an absolute requirement for union with God. This union cannot be wrought without a complete separation of the memory from all forms that are not God."[19]

Instead of striving to remember all that we have to do, we should turn our memory toward God like an open and empty bowl, so that he himself can fill it with everything we need to know to do his will.

> As a result all the operations of the memory and other faculties in this state are divine. God now possesses the faculties as their complete Lord, because of their transformation in Him. And consequently it is He Who divinely moves and commands them according to His spirit and will. As a result the operations are not different from those of God; but those the soul performs are of God and are divine operations. Since he who is united with God is one spirit with Him, as Saint Paul says (1 Cor 6:17), the operations of the soul united with God are of the divine Spirit and are divine.[20]

This is not merely speculation, but concrete reality. In this state one lives on a plane that is completely different from the normal one (which is actually abnormal). Saint John of the Cross gives concrete examples.

> A person will ask a soul in this state for prayers. The soul will not remember to carry out this request

---

[19] John of the Cross, *Ascent of Mount Carmel*, III, 2, 4, p. 215.
[20] Ibid., 8, pp. 216–17.

through any form or idea of that person remaining in the memory. If it is expedient to pray for him (that is, if God wants to receive prayer for this person), God will move its will and impart a desire to do so; at times God will give it a desire to pray for others whom it has never known nor heard of.

The reason is that God alone moves these souls to do those works that are in harmony with His will and ordinance, and they cannot be moved toward others. Thus the works and prayer of these souls always produce their effect.[21]

This helps to explain the Gospel text, which perhaps seems puzzling to us: "Whatever you ask in my name, I will do it" (Jn 14:13). To pray in Jesus' name is to pray inspired by his Spirit. When it is the Spirit himself who inspires the prayer, it is not unusual that it is heard. "[The Lord] had promised me", writes Teresa of Avila in her autobiography, "that there wasn't anything I might ask Him that He wouldn't do; that He already knew I wouldn't ask for anything other than what was in conformity with His glory."[22] But it is not only in the supernatural sphere that God leads a person, not only in the context of prayer. God's guidance also extends to daily life with its work and occupations. "Another example", continues John of the Cross: "At a particular time a per-

---

[21] Ibid., 10, p. 217.

[22] Teresa of Avila, *The Book of Her Life*, Collected Works of Saint Teresa of Avila, vol. 1 (Washington D.C.: ICS Publications, Institute of Carmelite Studies, 1976), p. 267.

son will have to attend to a necessary business matter. He will not remember through any form, but, without his knowing how, the time and suitable way of attending to it will be impressed on his soul without fail."[23] We must not forget that these examples concern people who are in the "state of union". Saint John admits that even among such people "a person will hardly be found whose union with God is so continuous that his faculties, without any form, are always divinely moved, nevertheless there are those who are very habitually moved by God."[24]

But we do not need to wait until we have reached the state of union. We can begin long before that to learn how to live under the guidance of the Holy Spirit. "God must place the soul in this supernatural state. Nevertheless, an individual must insofar as possible prepare himself. This he can do naturally with God's help."[25] How will he be able to do this? "By negation and emptiness of forms".[26] In other words, by using the faculty of memory in a less and less active and self-willed way and letting it be activated by God instead.

Naturally, this is only possible and meaningful for one who has a living relationship with God. As long as God has not become a reality in one's life, it is futile to expect any concrete guidance from him. A

[23] John of the Cross, *Ascent of Mount Carmel*, p. 217.
[24] Ibid., 16, p. 219.
[25] Ibid., 13, p. 218.
[26] Ibid.

God who is not real cannot give real impulses. Saint John of the Cross says explicitly that he is not referring to beginners here but to those who have arrived at "contemplation".[27] There are more of these people than one might believe, people who recognize themselves and breathe a sigh of relief when they read his description of the third sign: "A person likes to remain alone in loving awareness of God, without particular considerations, in interior peace and quiet and repose, and without the acts and exercises . . . of the intellect, memory and will."[28] These are people whose house is already somewhat at rest, that is, who have "mortified and silenced the appetites".[29] They are no longer completely torn by their conflicting appetites, but have begun to recollect their powers and direct them to God.

It is obvious that one cannot leave behind one's natural way of living in one day. It is a long process. One cannot expect God to take all the initiative as long as surrender is not total. Within the charismatic movement, one sometimes turns the responsibility over to God a little too soon. It is possible that openness to the Holy Spirit can then, in practice, be confused with openness to one's unconscious and its impulses. But the great merit of the charismatic movement is that it has taken the Holy Spirit seriously and reminded the Church that the Spirit is not

[27] Ibid., 2, 1–2, pp. 214–15.
[28] Ibid. II, 4, p. 141.
[29] Ibid., I, 15, 2, p. 105.

given to us for our enjoyment but to guide us and live in us.

Saint John of the Cross points out that in the end, our surrender may never serve as an excuse to neglect our duty. If God does not remind us about what we need to know, and if due to our inadequate surrender he does not yet use us completely as his instruments in the world, we ought to make use of our understanding and memory.[30] But the one who honestly tries to place his faculties at God's disposal notices that, in practice, it works better than he thought it would. As soon as one is completely abandoned to God, everything happens by itself. The one who has experienced this will no longer live in the old way.

Surrender and Our Own Activity

When we speak of surrender, we often hear the objection: "Does that mean we can no longer do anything ourselves? Can it be right to just sit and wait for God? Has he not given us an intellect and a will so that we will use them? Could this 'total surrender' not lead to laziness and apathy?" The simplest way to answer this is by turning to Jesus. "I do nothing on my own authority but speak thus as the Father taught me" (Jn 8:28). Do we get the impression that this makes him idle, that he takes it easy while letting the Father do all the work, or is it precisely this total surrender that

[30] Ibid., III, 15, 1, p. 235.

is the secret of the zeal that consumes him for the Father's glory (Jn 2:17)? Is it not the Father who drives him from town to town to speak about love? Doing nothing oneself does *not* mean that one does nothing at all. It is just the opposite, but one does not do it alone. "And he who sent me is with me; he has not left me alone, for I always do what is pleasing to him" (Jn 8:29). It is always the Father and Jesus together as a duo, or rather as a Trinity: The Father as principle, Jesus as the Father's instrument, and the Spirit as the Father's driving force. All three are completely involved: the Father in taking the initiative, the Spirit in driving and leading Jesus according to the Father's directive, and Jesus in accepting the Spirit's guidance and so fulfilling the Father's will.

Thus everything a person does ought to have a Trinitarian quality. One should do it, not alone, as an independent creature, but as incorporated into the Son and, therefore, like him and with him, the Father's instrument, activated by the Spirit. An activity that bears this Trinitarian mark is necessarily more fruitful and more "effective" than a self-willed activity. That is why it is naïve to believe that surrender leads to apathy. It is exactly the opposite. Surrender increases one's potential.

It is not activity as such that is opposed to surrender, since God himself prompts us to activity. What is incompatible with surrender is impulsive, self-governed activity. "Natural activity", writes de Caussade, "is the enemy of abandonment. . . . It prevents, obstructs or spoils all the operations of grace and substitutes, in the soul which succumbs to it, the impulsion of the human spirit for that of the divine Spirit. In fact there is no doubt that the impetuosity with which we give ourselves up to good works proceeds from a hidden source of self-confidence, and a thoughtless presumption that makes us imagine that we are doing or can do great things."[31] *Natural* activity does not take the words of Jesus seriously: "Apart from me you can do nothing" (Jn 15:5). Saint Paul, on the other hand, was convinced that he must let go of all his own strength in order to let God's strength work in him. When the Lord says: "My grace is sufficient for you, for my power is made perfect in weakness", he responds with: "I will all the more gladly boast of my weaknesses, that the power of Christ may rest upon me. . . . For when I am weak, then I am strong" (2 Cor 12:9-10).

Active or Passive?

When God leads us to activity, we let ourselves be led, and then an activity arises that bears his imprint. Is this activity or passivity? It is actually passive activity. Father de Caussade speaks of "a free and active cooperation [with God]" that is at the same time "infused and mystical".[32] Let us give an example. You

---

[31] De Caussade, Letters, *Abandonment to Divine Providence*, p. 198.
[32] De Caussade, *Abandonment to Divine Providence*, p. 54.

must write an important letter, and you want to do it as God's instrument in a spirit of complete surrender. Thoughts may come to you without your having to think yourself; you are "inspired", it is just given to you. But God may also activate your intellect and make you think yourself. Surrender consists then in thinking yourself, not in a self-willed way, but prompted by him. This kind of thinking is marked by calmness and relaxation. You do not wrinkle your forehead or clench your teeth. In the midst of active thinking, you are passive. "The good pleasure of God makes use of us in two ways", writes de Caussade: "either it compels us to perform certain actions, or it simply works within us."[33] But for the individual, it is always the same: total surrender.

Can we abandon ourselves too much? Can we exaggerate surrender? Surrender is an essential element in love, and when it comes to love we can never exaggerate, just the opposite. We are always indebted in love. "Owe no one anything, except to love one another" (Rom 13:8). If surrender leads to laxity, it is not because the surrender was too radical, but because one surrendered oneself to one's egoism instead of to God. To surrender oneself to God, who is self-giving love and pure commitment, cannot but lead to greater eagerness and a renewed and committed love. We see it with the prophet Elias in his double motto:

[33] Ibid., p. 52.

"The Lord lives in whose sight I stand" (1 Kings 17:1 Vulgate), and "with zeal have I been zealous for the Lord God of hosts" (ibid., 19:10, 14). The second motto is a consequence of the first one: it is because he keeps himself before the face of God that he has received something of God's zeal.

De Caussade is never afraid of going too far with surrender, and no one can dispute his expertise in this area. He even dares to say that complete surrender is not possible if one continues to act by the virtues.[34] He continues: "[The Bride] prefers to wander without order or method in abandoning herself to His [the Bridegroom's] guidance rather than to endeavor to gain confidence by following the beaten tracks of virtue. Let us go to God, then my soul, in abandonment, and let us acknowledge that we are incapable of acquiring virtue by our own industry or effort; but let us not allow this absence of particular virtues to diminish our confidence."[35] This may seem risky, perhaps, but it is really no more than Augustine's often quoted "Ama et fac quod vis" (love and do what you will).

This total surrender presupposes an equally total asceticism, an asceticism that is at the same time more demanding but less difficult than those penances we can read about in traditional pious literature. It is more

[34] Ibid., p. 75.
[35] Ibid.

demanding, because one must continually give up all one's own plans and desires. Everything must be offered at every moment. But it is still less difficult, since the offering is a step into God's rest (Heb 4:3). It is infinitely liberating not to *have to* stand on one's own two feet, to be *allowed* to be God's child and play before his face. Yes, life becomes more and more play. "Your children have only to love You without ceasing, and to fulfill their small duties like children. A child on its mother's lap is occupied only with its games as if it has nothing else to do but play with its mother."[36] De Caussade explains further how God, in his goodness, arranges that what is the most necessary on the natural plane is also easy and light. Nothing is as necessary as breathing, sleeping, and eating, but neither is anything as easy. It must be the same on the supernatural plane. The most important thing we have to do on that plane is to love. Therefore it must be easy to love.[37] Everyone who tries and who crosses the threshold discovers, to his great amazement, that it is much easier to love than not to love.

Peace of Heart

The total surrender of our whole self and all of our faculties to God presupposes that we have peace of

[36] Ibid.
[37] Ibid., p. 4.

heart. Letting ourselves be led by God's spirit in everything we do is possible only if we are on God's wavelength, that is, if we have peace, for our God is a God of peace (1 Cor 14:33). We do not hear God when we have unrest in our souls; we do not perceive his inspirations when we have a restless heart. "The great principle of the interior life", writes de Caussade,

> is the peace of the soul, and it must be preserved with such care that the moment it is attacked all else must be put aside and every effort made to try and regain this holy peace, just as, in an outbreak of fire, everything else is neglected to hasten to extinguish the flames. . . . The devil does not fail to take advantage. For this reason he uses all his cunning to deprive us of peace, and under a thousand specious pretexts, at one time about self-examination, or sorrow for sin, at another about the way we continually neglect grace, or that by our own fault we make no progress; that God will, at last, forsake us, and a hundred other devices from which very few people can defend themselves. This is why masters of the spiritual life lay down this great principle to distinguish the true inspirations of God from those that emanate from the devil; that the former are always sweet and peaceful inducing to confidence and humility, while the latter are intense, restless, and violent, leading to discouragement and mistrust, or else to presumption and self-will. We must, therefore, constantly reject all that does not show signs of peace, submission,

sweetness and confidence, all of which bear, as it were, the impression of the seal of God.[38]

A great help in preserving and increasing this inner peace is striving to work in a calm, relaxed, and self-controlled way. Stress is often a sign of an all too obtrusive presence of one's own ego. God is never a stress factor. Every person has his own rhythm, and it is important to respect that. Those who do violence to it without good reason distance themselves from God. If one is in disharmony with oneself, one cannot be in harmony with God. Calm, peace, and relaxation do not have to do only with bodily or physical well-being. They create a greater openness to God, and at the same time they incarnate God's peace within us, the peace that, Paul writes, must "reign" in our hearts (1 Col 3:15).

The Prayer of Surrender

Total surrender should be our fundamental attitude. We ought to pray, work, speak, and rest with this attitude. We may not take a vacation from this surrender. It is actually, in itself, a constant vacation! But prayer is nevertheless a privileged opportunity to practice this fundamental attitude. During our work we so easily become self-important; the self-willed ego slips in unnoticed and ruins everything. It takes

---

[38] Ibid., pp. 142–43.

a long time before we learn to preserve a selfless attitude in our work. We work with our body, of course,
and it has its bad habits. The restlessness of our nerves
affects and influences our heart, also. At prayer, on
the other hand, our body is at rest, and it can even
help in deepening our surrender.

There is a prayer that we can call the prayer of surrender. In this prayer it is not I who prays; I let God
pray in me. The only thing I have to do is remain in
God's light. Saint John of the Cross calls this prayer
"contemplation", and he defines it precisely as God's
prayer in us: "For contemplation is nothing else than
a secret and peaceful and loving inflow of God, which,
if not hampered, fires the soul in the spirit of love."[39]
How does one hinder this divine inflow? By thinking and talking and by taking the initiative oneself,
by excessively showing one's good will. To a sister
who complains that she is less recollected at prayer
than during her work, de Caussade says: "God deprives you of feelings of devotion during prayer, to
prevent the desires and eagerness they give rise to.
While you are at prayer remain exactly as you are in
solitude. I do not exact from you an atom more of
application or attention. Continue in this thoughtful
pensive state without allowing your thoughts to dwell
on created things and then you will be in God without

[39] John of the Cross, *Dark Night of the Soul*, 6, in *Collected Works*,
p. 318.

understanding how, without feeling His presence, nor even knowing how this can be."[40]

Our only concern in this state ought to be: to find ourselves in the flood of God's light, so that he can reach us. We can learn from Saint John of the Cross how this is done. In this area he is one of the greatest experts in the history of the Church.

> The attitude necessary in the night of sense [one could say: in this total surrender] is to pay no attention to discursive meditation, since this is not the time for it. They should allow the soul to remain in rest and quietude, even though it may seem very obvious to them that they are doing nothing and wasting time, and even though they think this disinclination to think about anything is due to their laxity. Through patience and perseverance in prayer, they will be doing a great deal without activity on their part. All that is required of them here is freedom of soul, that they liberate themselves from the impediment and fatigue of ideas and thoughts and care not about thinking and meditation. They must be content simply with a loving and peaceful attentiveness to God, and live without concern, without the effort, and without the desire to taste or feel Him. All these desires disquiet the soul and distract it from the peaceful quiet and sweet idleness of the contemplation which is being communicated to it.[41]

[40] De Caussade, Letters, *Abandonment to Divine Providence*, p. 238.
[41] John of the Cross, *Dark Night of the Soul*, 10, 4, p. 317.

We have already said that in some way life becomes play. Even prayer becomes play. One should go to prayer, writes Saint John of the Cross, as though "remaining in ease and freedom of spirit".[42]

One cannot, of course, experience this well-being and freedom at *all times*. This prayer of surrender can be dry and dull. But it is actually self-love that finds it boring, and that is, of course, good! Self-love must be so bored and desperate that it finally dies of it. "But what am I to do?" writes a sister in desperation to Father de Caussade. "Nothing, nothing my daughter, but to let God act, and to be careful not to obstruct by an inopportune activity the operation of God; to abstain even from sensible acts of resignation, except when you feel God requires them of you. Remain then like a block of wood, and you will see later the marvels that God will have worked during that silent night of inaction."[43]

A Testimony: Letting Go

Everything that has been said about surrender can be summed up in the following testimony of a priest.

For years, which seemed like centuries, I had a dream, even as a small boy:

[42] Ibid., 5, p. 318.
[43] De Caussade, Letters, *Abandonment to Divine Providence*, p. 359.

I sat completely alone on the earth.
Completely alone.
I saw myself sitting on that great globe.
Then it began. The constantly recurring
dreadful anguish.
The globe began to spin with raging speed.
The trees cracked. The mountains collapsed.
The ocean washed up out of the deep.
The wind howled in my ears: Let go! Let go! Let go!
I did not let go. I clung to the earth
with mouth and hands and feet.
For I was afraid. What will become of me
in this void, in this empty night?
Never, never . . .

Until I awoke. Wet from perspiration and anguish.

Now I am thirty-nine years old. I have let go. It was about six years ago. It happened, not in a dream, but during the day, in the midst of reality, and I felt: now I am finished, now anything can happen. Sorrow or joy, anything! I loosened my grasp. I surrendered myself to God's will in something that became increasingly clearer, something that was a matter of life and death. I was dragged along into emptiness. I lost my bearings and my foothold. Such an experience can drive one insane. One could take one's own life. Everything becomes foreign to you. You really feel you have lost your grip. Lost. You must be saved, born anew out of blood and darkness.

And when it has come to this point, everything becomes new, even a flower, a butterfly, or the billowing of the wind in the reeds.

But most of all Him.

It is truly a matter of all or nothing. It is heaven or hell for a person. One becomes a person or an inhuman creature. You stand before the grace-filled choice, particularly after the Incarnation of the Son. Once! One realizes later that life was pointing toward this all along, as the Old Covenant toward the New, as the night toward the day, as losing life toward gaining it.

I write this for those who know it, so that they may rejoice with me in the Lord, and for those who are confronted with it, so that they will not turn back, for the Lord is also shepherd in the night. He leads you through dark valleys, and your heart can only come to the place for which it longs through dark valleys.

A hurricane of love is raging over the earth, with his tugging, luring, shouting: Let go, give in, in God's name give in, all of you together.[44]

---

[44] Flor Hofmans (1925–1964), Flemish priest, professor in theology in Santiago de Chile.